The Life of Christ Jesus

Chris Morais

Published by Chris Morais, 2024.

THE LIFE OF CHRIST JESUS

First edition. Oct 27, 2024.

Copyright © 2024 Chris Morais.

Also by Chris Morais

Kidney Cancer
The Life of Christ Jesus

Table of Contents

Preface 1

THE PROPHETIC FOUNDATIONS OF CHRIST'S BIRTH 3

Introduction 4

In the Beginning 6

The Prophecy of the Virgin Birth 8

The Prophecy of the Birthplace 10

The Prophecy about the Voice 12

The Conception of the Voice 14

The Annunciation 16

The Visitation 18

The Birth of the Voice 20

The Concern of Joseph 22

The Census and the Journey to Bethlehem 24

THE BIRTH AND THE STRUGGLE FOR SURVIVAL 26

Introduction 27

The Birth 29

The First Christmas Celebration 33

The Presentation 35

The Visit of the Magi 37

The Flight to Egypt 39

Return to Nazareth from Egypt 41

THE SILENT YEARS 43

Introduction 45

The Boy in the Temple 47

The First Phase of Silent Years 49

Mary and Joseph's Parenting 51

The Carpenter's Son 53

Was Jesus Married? 55

The Brothers of Jesus 58

BREAKING THE SILENCE 60

Introduction 61

The Voice Prepares the Way 63

The Baptism 65

The Temptation 67

THE PUBLIC MINISTRY 69

Introduction 71

The Chosen Twelve 74

The Sermon on the Mount 77

The Teachings 79

Redefining the Law 81

Teaching to Pray 84

The Miracles 86

The Parables 88

The Transfiguration 90

The Triumphal Entry 92

THE PASSION WEEK 94

Introduction 95

Cleansing of the Temple 97

Confrontations with Religious Leaders 99

Teaching in the Temple 101

The Olivet Discourse 103

A Friend Agrees to Betray 105

The Last Supper 107

In the Garden of Gethsemane 109

The Betrayal and Arrest 111

The Condemnation 113

The Denial of Peter 115

Trial before Pilate 117

Sent to Herod 119

Sentenced to Death 121

The Torture 123

The Crucifixion 125

AT THE CROSS 127

Introduction... 128

Forgiving the Persecutors 130

Soldiers Casting Lots for His Clothes 132

The Penitent Thief 133

Jesus and His Mother 135

Agony at the Cross... 138

It is Finished... 140

The Restoration 143

The Death Certificate 145

The Son of God Indeed 148

THE RESURRECTION AND ASCENSION 150

Introduction... 151

In the Tomb.. 153

Defeating Death 155

The Appearances 157

The Greatest Skeptic Ever Lived 160

Barbecue at the Beach 163

Choosing a Successor 165

The Great Commission 167

The Goodbye	169
The Promise of the Second Coming	171
Establishing His Identity	173
Epilogue: The Journey Continues	175
A Note	177

Preface

Embarking on the journey to explore the Life of Christ, we immerse into a narrative that has shaped history, transformed lives, and offered hope across generations. This story, deeply rooted in historical events, transcends the confines of time and geography, speaking directly to the hearts and minds of all who encounter it. It is more than just a story—it is the quintessential story of all time.

In this book, "The Life of Christ Jesus," I embark on a profound exploration of the most pivotal figure in human history. Jesus Christ, whose teachings have altered landscapes, whose life has inspired countless, and whose death and resurrection remain at the very heart of Christian faith, is the central figure of our study.

By weaving together the Gospel accounts in a chronological narrative and citing verses from the New International Version (NIV), this book presents a comprehensive exploration of the life of Jesus Christ. From the prophecies that foretold His coming to the miraculous events of His birth, from His challenging teachings and compassionate miracles to His agonizing crucifixion and victorious resurrection, each chapter offers insights into His profound identity and mission. Through these pages, you will discover a figure who was both divine and human.

I clarify some common misconceptions and skepticisms, such as the virgin birth, the Roman census, the brothers of Jesus, whether Jesus was married, and whether Jesus ever claimed to be God, among others. The aim is to reaffirm believers' faith and challenge skeptics by demonstrating the credibility of Christ's claims and their centrality to a fulfilled and purposeful life.

CHRIS MORAIS

As you journey through this book, it is my hope that you will encounter Jesus in a way that is refreshing and transformative. May the chapters that unfold deepen your faith and broaden your understanding of the One who calls us to follow Him. Whether you are exploring the life of Christ for the first time or revisiting His story with years of faith behind you, may this book serve as a valuable resource in your spiritual journey. This book is crafted for believers who seek to deepen their understanding of their Savior, and for skeptics who may question the historical and theological claims about Jesus.

The Life of Christ Jesus is a story that refuses to be confined to the pages of history; it is alive, active, and utterly relevant to the challenges and questions of our contemporary world. Embark on this journey with an open heart, and discover the enduring truth of Jesus Christ, whose life continues to inspire and challenge us to live out the greatness of His love. May you discover that Jesus is the promised Messiah, the Son of God, who came to save humanity from sin and death. May this exploration deepen your understanding, strengthen your faith, and inspire you to live in a way that reflects the love, grace, and truth of Jesus Christ.

Chris Morais, MSc, MPhil, PhD

THE PROPHETIC FOUNDATIONS OF CHRIST'S BIRTH

This section covers the following topics:

- *Introduction*
- *In the Beginning*
- *The Prophecy of the Virgin Birth*
- *The Prophecy of the Birthplace*
- *The Prophecy about the Voice*
- *The Conception of the Voice*
- *The Annunciation*
- *The Visitation*
- *The Birth of the Voice*
- *The Concern of Joseph*
- *The Census and the Journey to Bethlehem*

Introduction

The story of Jesus Christ is unlike any other. Often called the greatest story ever told, His life marks a testament to His unique mission and divine nature. The birth of Jesus Christ stands as a monumental event in human history. There was never anyone like Him before, and there will never be again. His birth was not just an ordinary event; it was the fulfillment of precise prophecies, unfolding exactly when and how it was meant to, for the ultimate salvation of humanity.

The prophecy from Isaiah, which says a virgin will conceive and give birth to a son named Immanuel (Isaiah 7:14), is not just a statement but a powerful sign of Jesus' divine entry into the world. Similarly, Micah's prophecy pinpoints Bethlehem as the birthplace of the Messiah (Micah 5:2), underlining not only the place but also its deep historical and spiritual significance. Additionally, the prophets Isaiah and Malachi spoke about John the Baptist, the voice in the wilderness, who would prepare the way for Jesus' ministry.

After the prophetic announcements, there was a significant silence—historically known as the 400-year intertestamental period. This silence was dramatically broken with the announcement of John the Baptist's conception to Zechariah. This event sets the stage for a sequence of miraculous happenings: the Annunciation by the angel Gabriel to Mary that she would bear the Son of God, Mary's visitation to her cousin Elizabeth, and Joseph's struggles upon discovering Mary's pregnancy. The journey to Bethlehem for the census solidifies the fulfillment of prophecies concerning the Messiah's birthplace.

Let us begin by exploring these extraordinary events surrounding the birth of Christ—each foretold by prophets and fulfilled with divine precision, reinforcing the truth of God's word and His plan for humanity's redemption.

In the Beginning

The story of humanity's interaction with the divine starts in the perfection of the Garden of Eden. Here, God placed Adam and Eve in a paradise where they had everything they could wish for, except for one forbidden fruit. This prohibition was not just an arbitrary rule; it was a critical choice that would define humanity forever.

God's creation of humans was not about making beings without the ability to think or choose for themselves. Instead, He gave Adam and Eve the freedom to make their own choices, emphasizing that with freedom comes responsibility. Initially, they lived in perfect harmony with God—direct, unbroken communion.

However, this harmony was shattered when Satan, disguised as a serpent, brought doubt and deceit into this clear relationship. He tempted Adam and Eve to disobey God's command, leading to the first sin—a choice that had monumental consequences for all of humanity. This act introduced a deep-seated separation between humans and God, illustrated by Adam and Eve hiding behind makeshift coverings of leaves.

In the aftermath of this sin, God pronounced a curse on the serpent, but within that curse was a prophecy full of hope. "And I will put enmity between you and the woman, and between your offspring and hers; he will crush your head, and you will strike his heel." (Genesis 3:15). He promised a battle between the serpent's offspring and the woman's, culminating in a victory over sin and death. This prophecy is not just about Eve but points to a future woman—Mary—and her offspring, Jesus Christ. The "striking of the heel" refers to Jesus' crucifixion, a temporary victory for Satan, and the "crushing of the head" symbolizes Jesus' ultimate victory over sin and death.

This early promise in Genesis is not just a small part of the story. It sets the stage for the entire narrative of redemption that runs through Scripture, leading up to Jesus' life and ministry. It even hints at the virgin birth prophesied by Isaiah about 700 years later, showcasing God's master plan to fix the broken relationship between Him and humanity.

This foundational prophecy is key in understanding how deeply and perfectly God planned every detail of Jesus' life—a life that would bring hope and restoration to a fallen world.

The Prophecy of the Virgin Birth

Long before the world experienced the miracle of Jesus' birth, the prophet Isaiah delivered a powerful message that has echoed through the ages, lighting up periods of darkness with hope. He declared, "Therefore the Lord himself will give you a sign: The virgin will conceive and give birth to a son, and will call him Immanuel" (Isaiah 7:14). This was not just a simple prediction; it was a divine promise, a key moment in God's grand plan for humanity. It told of a miraculous event: a child born to a virgin, an idea both miraculous and central to the Christian faith.

Now, it is important to address some controversy surrounding Isaiah's prophecy about the virgin birth. Critics sometimes argue that the original Hebrew word in the prophecy might mean 'unmarried young woman' rather than 'virgin.' This discussion questions the accuracy of the narrative concerning Mary's virgin birth. However, this interpretation does not weaken the prophecy's miraculous nature; rather, it underscores how precisely God communicates His intentions.

To really understand this, let us look at the cultural norms of Isaiah's time. Back then, society had strict views on sexuality and marriage. An unmarried young woman would almost definitely be a virgin by the standards of her community. The societal norms reinforced this. So, when Isaiah talks about an unmarried young woman conceiving, the implication of her virginity fits perfectly with the societal expectations. By using terms that matched the culture yet predicted something extraordinary, Isaiah's prophecy spans centuries to fulfill itself in the New Testament without losing its core message.

THE LIFE OF CHRIST JESUS

Understanding this context bridges any gaps between skepticism and faith by showing how the prophecy and its fulfillment through Mary's conception of Jesus align flawlessly. This perfect match reaffirms the prophecy's validity and its important role in the larger story of redemption. The virgin birth stands as a clear testament to the divine intersecting with the human realm, a miracle predicted with intention and realized in a way that leaves no doubt about its importance.

Think about the uniqueness of Jesus' birth prophecy. We remember many historical figures for their actions, but Jesus is unique because His arrival was foretold with remarkable specificity, long before it occurred. Unlike vague predictions that might fit many situations, this prophecy specifies unique details—like the virgin birth—that clearly distinguish it. It is not just accurate; it is precise, telling us that something extraordinary, something divine was about to happen.

And the story does not stop with just one prophecy. Another prediction, equally precise, tells us about the exact location of Jesus' birth. This further prophecy builds on what Isaiah said, adding more detail to God's carefully laid plan for salvation. It acts as another key piece in understanding the exceptional circumstances surrounding the birth of Jesus.

The Prophecy of the Birthplace

While the prophecy of the virgin birth is extraordinary, the specific location prophesied for this event is just as incredible. This child, destined to change history, was foretold to be born in Bethlehem, a seemingly insignificant town within the vast Roman Empire. Despite its obscurity, Bethlehem was divinely chosen for the birth of Jesus, showcasing the exactness with which God's promises are fulfilled.

This prophecy is detailed in the book of Micah. Centuries before Jesus' birth, Micah 5:2 states, 'But you, Bethlehem Ephrathah, though you are small among the clans of Judah, out of you will come for me one who will be ruler over Israel, whose origins are from of old, from ancient times.' This not only pinpoints the location but also highlights the eternal origins of the Messiah—'from of old, from ancient times'—emphasizing the deep-rooted divine plan.

The choice of Bethlehem is steeped in rich symbolism. Its Hebrew meaning, "house of bread," beautifully correlates with Jesus' later declaration in the Gospel of John, "I am the bread of life" (John 6:35). This is not just a coincidence but a deliberate part of God's design, portraying Jesus as the spiritual nourishment for a world in desperate need of redemption and truth.

Moreover, Bethlehem's significance is enhanced by its association with King David, establishing a lineage that meets the messianic expectation of a descendant from David. As detailed in the Gospel of Matthew, this lineage directly links Jesus to David, both originating from the same modest town, thus securing Jesus' integral role in the grand narrative of redemption that spans both Old and New Testaments.

THE LIFE OF CHRIST JESUS

The selection of Bethlehem for the Nativity story also speaks powerfully about the nature of God's kingdom. It sharply contrasts with human expectations of majesty and power, instead offering a vision of humility, simplicity, and connection with the marginalized. Jesus' birth in such humble circumstances overturns worldly ideas of greatness and power, providing a strong critique of societal norms and values.

Mentioning Bethlehem in the Nativity story also adds a layer of historical credibility to the Gospel narratives. The account of Mary and Joseph traveling to Bethlehem, in line with a Roman census, aligns well with known historical practices, reinforcing the reliability of the Gospel of Luke and addressing doubts about the historicity of these events. This aspect will be explored further in the section 'The Birth and the Struggle for Survival'.

The story continues beyond the prophecy of Jesus' birthplace, unfolding with the announcement of John the Baptist, the Voice, whose own foretold arrival sets the stage for Jesus' ministry. This sequence of divine predictions and their fulfillment underscores not only the precision of biblical prophecy but also the intricate planning and faithfulness of God in orchestrating the backdrop for the arrival of His Son.

The Prophecy about the Voice

The scriptures richly detail the prophecies not just of Jesus' birthplace, but also of a key figure who would precede Him: a herald whose task was to prepare the way for the Messiah. This figure, brought to life through the vivid and precise words of prophets like Isaiah and Malachi, plays a pivotal role in setting the stage for the arrival of Jesus.

Isaiah introduces us to this figure as a voice calling in the wilderness, compellingly urging preparation for the coming Lord: "A voice of one calling: 'In the wilderness prepare the way for the Lord; make straight in the desert a highway for our God'" (Isaiah 40:3). This prophecy sketches the portrait of a man who would lay the spiritual groundwork, calling on people to ready their hearts and minds for the one who would bring ultimate salvation.

Adding further depth, Malachi describes this precursor as a messenger sent ahead of the Lord: "I will send my messenger, who will prepare the way before me. Then suddenly the Lord you are seeking will come to his temple; the messenger of the covenant, whom you desire, will come," says the Lord Almighty (Malachi 3:1). This prediction not only emphasizes the messenger's crucial role but also the dramatic, sudden appearance of the Lord in His temple—a moment filled with messianic anticipation and divine encounter.

These prophecies find their fulfillment in John the Baptist, who is both the voice in the wilderness and the preparatory messenger. John's mission was marked by a call to repentance and baptism, effectively preparing the way for Jesus. After His baptism, Jesus famously entered the temple and began to teach, even reading from the scroll in a scene that fulfills Isaiah's prophecy about the anointed one who would bring good news to the poor and set the oppressed free (Luke 4:17-21). The pinpoint accuracy and specific details of these prophecies are not just impressive—they show a divine orchestration at work.

John the Baptist further solidified his identity during a telling encounter with religious leaders, as recorded in the Gospel of John, Chapter 1. Questioned about his identity, John firmly denied being the Messiah and instead embraced his role as prophesied by Isaiah: "I am the voice of one calling in the wilderness, 'Make straight the way for the Lord'" (John 1:23). This was not merely a rejection of any personal acclaim but a powerful confirmation of his mission to prepare the path for Jesus' ministry. John's clear understanding of his role as the herald, not the hero, underlines the truth of the Biblical prophecies and their remarkable fulfillment, presenting a strong case for the reliability and divine inspiration of the scriptures.

Thus, the scriptural narrative intricately interweaves the prophecies concerning the Messiah's birth, the place of His birth, and the herald who would announce His coming. The precision with which these events were predicted and came to pass speaks volumes about the detailed and deliberate nature of God's plan for redemption, established centuries before they occurred.

The years following Malachi's prophecy, known as the intertestamental period or the "silent years," spanned about 400 years during which no new prophetic voices emerged. This silence was profound, marking a period of waiting and anticipation for the fulfillment of God's longstanding promises. The silence was finally broken with the angelic announcement of John the Baptist's conception to Zechariah, signaling that the long-awaited time to fulfill these ancient prophecies had finally arrived.

The Conception of the Voice

After the prophecies of Isaiah and Micah, there followed a significant period of approximately 400 years of prophetic silence, until the narrative resumed with the divine announcement of John the Baptist's birth to Zechariah, heralding the fulfillment of these ancient promises.

Zechariah, a priest from the division of Abijah, was performing his sacred duties in the temple when he was startled by the appearance of the angel Gabriel beside the altar of incense. Gabriel, bringing a message of comfort and joy, told Zechariah, "Do not be afraid, Zechariah; your prayer has been heard. Your wife Elizabeth will bear you a son, and you are to call him John" (Luke 1:13). This moment was pivotal, tying Zechariah and Elizabeth directly to God's plan of salvation.

Gabriel explained that John would be great before the Lord, filled with the Holy Spirit from birth, and destined to turn many back to God (Luke 1:15-16). He was to be the prophesied voice in the wilderness, as Isaiah envisioned (Isaiah 40:3), and the messenger foretold by Malachi who would precede the coming of the Lord (Malachi 3:1).

Zechariah's initial skepticism—how could such an event happen to them in their old age?—resulted in him being struck mute, a divine sign ensuring the truth of Gabriel's words. He would not speak again until the prophecies came to fruition with John's birth (Luke 1:20).

Elizabeth's pregnancy, following years of barrenness, stood as a testament to God's power to bring life where none seemed possible. In her seclusion, Elizabeth recognized God's hand at work, expressing her deep faith and gratitude by saying, "The Lord has done this for me" (Luke 1:25).

THE LIFE OF CHRIST JESUS

Gabriel's role was not finished with Zechariah and Elizabeth. He had another vital mission—to go to Nazareth and deliver a message to Mary that would alter the course of history. This Annunciation to Mary was not merely news but a divine revelation that she would bear the Son of God, Jesus Christ. Let us explore this profound event further.

The Annunciation

The Annunciation marks a pivotal moment when the Angel Gabriel revealed to the Virgin Mary that she would conceive and give birth to Jesus Christ, the Son of God. This event signals the beginning of the Incarnation, where God manifests in human form. It stands as a profound testament to faith, obedience, and God's profound love for humanity. The Annunciation celebrates God's deliberate intervention in history, choosing a humble woman to facilitate an extraordinary plan. It reminds us that God often chooses the modest and the willing—those like Mary, who respond to His call with faith and obedience.

Luke's Gospel paints a vivid picture of this miraculous event. Gabriel, sent by God, greets Mary with words that honor and comfort her: "Greetings, you who are highly favored! The Lord is with you" (Luke 1:28). Though initially perplexed and troubled, Mary is reassured by Gabriel's words, "Do not be afraid, Mary; you have found favor with God" (Luke 1:30). Gabriel then unfolds God's remarkable plan: "You will conceive and give birth to a son, and you are to call him Jesus. He will be great and will be called the Son of the Most High" (Luke 1:31-32).

The implications of this announcement were profound. As a virgin engaged to Joseph, Mary faced potential severe social and personal repercussions due to her pregnancy. Understandably, Mary was both frightened and confused, prompting her to ask Gabriel, "How will this be, since I am a virgin?" Gabriel explained that her conception would be a divine act, beyond human comprehension: "The Holy Spirit will come on you, and the power of the Most High will overshadow you. So the holy one to be born will be called the Son of God" (Luke 1:35).

Mary's response to this divine revelation was exemplary. Despite the potential for social scorn and personal hardship, she accepted her role with immense faith and humility, stating, "I am the Lord's servant. May your word to me be fulfilled" (Luke 1:38). Her acceptance showcases not just her trust in God's plan but also her remarkable courage, serving as a model of faithfulness and obedience amidst uncertainty. This response underscores Mary's pivotal role in the salvation narrative, chosen for her purity and devotion, and it highlights the boundless power of God to orchestrate humanity's salvation through miraculous means.

Following this life-altering news, Gabriel shares another miracle with Mary: her relative Elizabeth has also conceived in her old age. With the knowledge that Elizabeth is six months along, Mary plans a visit to her cousin, leading to the next significant event—the Visitation.

The Visitation

One of the most touching events in the Bible is the story of the Visitation, where Mary, soon to be the mother of Jesus, visits her cousin Elizabeth. This event, rich with joy, prophecy, and the miraculous, occurs shortly after the angel Gabriel tells Mary about her divine pregnancy. Eager for support and kinship, Mary quickly travels to the hill country of Judea to see Elizabeth, who is also miraculously pregnant with John the Baptist despite her advanced age.

Upon Mary's arrival, a remarkable scene unfolds. As Mary greets her cousin, Elizabeth's baby leaps within her womb in joy. Filled with the Holy Spirit, Elizabeth exclaims loudly, "Blessed are you among women, and blessed is the child you will bear! But why am I so favored, that the mother of my Lord should come to me? As soon as the sound of your greeting reached my ears, the baby in my womb leaped for joy" (Luke 1:42-44). This extraordinary moment highlights not only the special nature of Mary's unborn child but also John's recognition of His divinity from the womb.

Elizabeth's response to Mary is both a blessing and an acknowledgment of Mary's steadfast faith: "Blessed is she who has believed that the Lord would fulfill his promises to her!" (Luke 1:45). This declaration recognizes Mary's belief in God's promise, setting a tone of faithfulness and trust that defines both women's experiences. Mary's reply to Elizabeth's greeting, known as the Magnificat, is a powerful hymn of praise to God. She exalts God for His favor, His mighty deeds, and His mercy, saying, "My soul glorifies the Lord and my spirit rejoices in God my Savior, for he has been mindful of the humble state of his servant. From now on all generations will call me blessed" (Luke 1:46-48). The

THE LIFE OF CHRIST JESUS

Magnificat captures Mary's deep faith and her recognition of God's actions in the world, celebrating His justice, mercy, and faithfulness.

The Visitation serves as a moment of mutual encouragement and prophetic confirmation. It brings together two women chosen by God to play crucial roles in the story of salvation. Elizabeth, the elder, offers blessings and affirmation to Mary, while Mary's visit provides joy and validation of Elizabeth's own miraculous pregnancy. This meeting symbolizes the convergence of the old and the new, as John the Baptist, a pivotal figure linking the prophetic traditions of the Old Testament with the New Covenant, rejoices in the presence of Jesus, who inaugurates the New Covenant.

As Mary and Elizabeth share in the joy of their miraculous circumstances, another person faces a profound challenge. Joseph, Mary's betrothed, grapples with confusion and concern over Mary's unexpected pregnancy. In a society where such news could lead to severe social stigma and personal trials, Joseph's predicament is deeply troubling. How could his virtuous fiancée be pregnant when they had not yet come together? This dilemma not only disturbs his heart but also casts doubt on their future together. Let us explore how faith and divine guidance help transform Joseph's doubt and fear into resolution and trust.

The Birth of the Voice

The Bible recounts the joy surrounding the birth of John, as Elizabeth's long period of barrenness was brought to an end. The arrival of her son not only filled her life with joy but also ended the disgrace associated with infertility in her community. Her neighbors and relatives rejoiced with her, acknowledging the Lord's mercy in this miraculous event.

The moment to name the newborn arrived on the eighth day, a significant event not only because of the circumcision but also for the naming itself. Tradition might have dictated naming him after his father, Zechariah, but Elizabeth, with a firm voice, declared, "He is to be called John" (Luke 1:60). This choice confounded those gathered, as the name 'John' was unfamiliar within their family lineage.

This scene also marked the moment of Zechariah's redemption. His muteness was not a punishment but a sign from God, highlighting the miraculous nature of the events unfolding. It was a dramatic demonstration to all that what was happening was divinely ordained. When the community sought Zechariah's input on the name, he asked for a writing tablet. His confirmation, "His name is John," instantly restored his speech, surprising everyone around. Zechariah's first actions were to praise God, a response that filled all present with awe.

The news of these events spread throughout the hill country of Judea, stirring curiosity and wonder among the people. The prevailing question on everyone's lips was, "What then is this child going to be?" The palpable sense of divine intervention was evident, indicating that John's life was set for a purpose ordained by Heaven (Luke 1:62-66).

Indeed, John grew, becoming strong in spirit, and he lived in the wilderness until the time came for him to make his public appearance

THE LIFE OF CHRIST JESUS

to Israel, marking the beginning of his crucial role as the forerunner to the Messiah.

The Concern of Joseph

In the story of Jesus' birth, Joseph, Mary's husband, often receives less attention, but his role is pivotal and his concerns show a deeply human aspect of the Christmas narrative. Imagine being Joseph: pledged to marry Mary, he discovers she is pregnant, and he knows he is not the father. This revelation must have been both shocking and bewildering, challenging his faith and love in profound ways.

The book of Matthew highlights Joseph's dilemma: "Because Joseph her husband was faithful to the law, and yet did not want to expose her to public disgrace, he had in mind to divorce her quietly" (Matthew 1:19). This verse reveals much about Joseph's character. Despite his personal pain and societal pressure, Joseph's primary concern was for Mary's well-being. At that time, a woman found to be pregnant out of wedlock could face severe repercussions. Joseph's decision to divorce her quietly was an act of compassion and protection, demonstrating his respect and care for Mary amid his own distress.

However, Joseph's situation takes a dramatic turn when an angel of the Lord appears to him in a dream, delivering a message that would change everything: "Joseph son of David, do not be afraid to take Mary home as your wife, because what is conceived in her is from the Holy Spirit. She will give birth to a son, and you are to give him the name Jesus, because he will save his people from their sins" (Matthew 1:20-21). This divine message provides clarity and direction at a crucial moment, reassuring Joseph that Mary's pregnancy is part of God's grand design and that he has a vital role to play.

Joseph's reaction to this heavenly guidance is a profound display of faith. Upon awakening, he does exactly as the angel instructed: he

THE LIFE OF CHRIST JESUS

takes Mary as his wife and accepts the role of earthly father to Jesus. This decision was not trivial; it required Joseph to trust in the angel's message and in God's overarching plan for salvation—a plan far beyond anything he could have imagined.

Joseph's story is a compelling element of the Christmas narrative because it illustrates the complexity of human emotions and the depth of faith needed to navigate them. His initial concern and his resolution to protect Mary, even at a personal cost, highlight his integrity and compassion. His openness to divine direction, changing his plans in response to God's messenger, reflects a deep trust in God, even against societal norms and expectations. Joseph's journey reminds us that faith often demands moving beyond our initial reactions, trusting in God's guidance even when the way forward is not clear.

Ultimately, Joseph's unwavering faith sets the stage for a commitment that alters the course of history. By choosing to support Mary and raise Jesus as his own, Joseph plays an essential role in the story of salvation.

With the earthly parents now united and the unborn Messiah cradled in Mary's womb, the stage is set for the next crucial event in this divine saga: the journey to Bethlehem.

The Census and the Journey to Bethlehem

The journey of Mary and Joseph to Bethlehem, prompted by a Roman census, stands as a critical moment in the narrative leading to the birth of Jesus Christ. While often mentioned briefly, this event carries immense significance as it aligns perfectly with ancient prophecies about the Messiah's birthplace.

The Bible records in the book of Luke, "In those days Caesar Augustus issued a decree that a census should be taken of the entire Roman world. And everyone went to their own town to register" (Luke 2:1-3). This decree, while a routine administrative act, served a higher divine purpose, bringing Mary and Joseph from Nazareth to Bethlehem. This was essential, as Joseph was of the house and line of David, thereby fulfilling the prophecy linking the Messiah directly to King David's lineage. The occurrence of this census is contested by skeptics, a topic I address in the next chapter.

The importance of Bethlehem as the birthplace of the Messiah was foretold by the Prophet Micah centuries earlier: "But you, Bethlehem Ephrathah, though you are small among the clans of Judah, out of you will come for me one who will be ruler over Israel" (Micah 5:2). This journey to Bethlehem was not just a fulfillment of legal requirements—it was a precise fulfillment of God's promises through the prophets, showcasing that God's plans, though often mysterious, are flawlessly timed and executed.

Mary and Joseph's obedience plays a pivotal role in this divine narrative. Despite the physical challenges of the journey—Mary being heavily pregnant and the potential hardships of travel possibly by donkey, which was a common mode of transport at the time—their commitment to God's plan is evident. Their trek, filled with discomfort and risks, particularly for Mary, underscores their faith and resilience. Their decision to adhere to God's guidance, amidst uncertainty, exemplifies a profound trust in divine providence.

Their participation in this divine plan accorded them an exceptional honor: serving as the earthly parents of Jesus, God incarnate. Mary is especially revered as the Mother of God or Theotokos, meaning "God Bearer." This title underscores her unique role in Christianity. Given Jesus' divinity, Mary's position as his mother is indeed significant and sacred. It is crucial to acknowledge this clear biblical truth without letting selective interpretations cloud this understanding.

Bethlehem represents more than just a geographical location; it symbolizes hope, prophecy fulfillment, and the profound truth of God's physical presence on Earth. On what seemed like an ordinary night in Bethlehem, something extraordinary happened that altered the course of history—the birth of Jesus, the Savior of the world. This moment, steeped in obedience and divine orchestration, highlights how pivotal events in God's plan often unfold through the humble compliance and courage of ordinary individuals.

THE BIRTH AND THE STRUGGLE FOR SURVIVAL

This section covers the following topics:

- *Introduction*
- *The Birth*
- *The First Christmas Celebration*
- *The Presentation*
- *The Visit of the Magi*
- *The Flight to Egypt*
- *Return to Nazareth from Egypt*

Introduction

I named this section 'The Birth and the Struggle for Survival' to underscore that, despite His divine nature as God incarnate and the Son of God, Jesus' childhood was fraught with danger and adversity. This section takes us through the early and tumultuous stages of Jesus Christ's life, a narrative rich with divine intervention, prophetic fulfillment, murderous threats, and profound human experiences. It begins with the miraculous birth of Jesus, an event that fulfills ancient prophecies and heralds God's promise of salvation.

The Birth marks not just the arrival of a baby but the incarnation of God Himself. This segment explores the humble and miraculous circumstances of Jesus' birth in Bethlehem, emphasizing its significance as the divine entrance of the Savior into human history.

The First Christmas Celebration not only reflects on the joy and worship surrounding Jesus' birth but also addresses the misconception that Christmas is a pagan practice, affirming its deep Christian roots.

The Presentation in the Temple follows, where Jesus, in accordance with Jewish law, is dedicated to God. This event features profound prophetic encounters with Simeon and Anna, who recognize the child as the Messiah and a light for revelation to the Gentiles, underscoring Jesus' significance not only to the Jews but to the entire world.

The Visit of the Magi introduces us to the wise men from the East, whose journey to worship Jesus signifies the recognition of His kingship and divinity by distant nations. Their gifts of gold, frankincense, and myrrh symbolize Jesus' roles as king, priest, and prophet, foreshadowing His ultimate sacrifice.

The Massacre of the Innocents and the Flight to Egypt recounts the darker side of His early life, where Herod's attempt to kill Jesus results in tragedy for many families in Bethlehem. This event fulfills the prophecies of Jeremiah and highlights the stark contrast between earthly power and divine purpose.

The subsequent flight to Egypt and eventual return to Nazareth illustrate God's providential protection over His Son, ensuring the fulfillment of His earthly mission. Each story is a mosaic piece of the grander narrative of redemption, emphasizing that Jesus' early life was marked by divine intervention and fulfillment of God's promises.

The Birth

The Bible describes the extraordinary night of Jesus' birth with deep reverence and awe. "While they were there [in Bethlehem], the time came for the baby to be born, and she [Mary] gave birth to her firstborn, a son. She wrapped him in cloths and placed him in a manger, because there was no guest room available for them" (Luke 2:6-7). This passage highlights both the simplicity and the majesty of the Nativity. Jesus, the King of Kings, was born not in a grand palace but in a humble stable, surrounded not by signs of earthly wealth but by an atmosphere of love and faith. His first bed was a manger, a simple feeding trough for animals.

On that silent and holy night, beneath a canopy of stars, the quiet town of Bethlehem witnessed a miraculous event that would alter the course of human history. A modest stable became the backdrop for the birth of Jesus Christ, the Savior of humanity. This moment, though humble in setting, was monumental in its implications, heralding a new era of hope and fulfilling God's promise to mankind.

This night—the birth of Jesus—was when Heaven touched Earth, introducing the divine into the human condition in the most humble and unexpected of ways. It marks the fulfillment of centuries of prophecy and the beginning of the greatest story ever told—the story of Jesus Christ. From the promise of a savior born of a woman in Genesis 3:15, to the specific prophecy of a virgin birth in Isaiah 7:14, and even the precise location of His birth in Bethlehem as predicted in Micah 5:2, every detail underscores a deliberate divine arrangement. These prophecies are not isolated promises; they are interconnected revelations that together disclose the breadth of God's plan for salvation, meticulously unfolding with the birth of Jesus. They affirm that the nativity is not just a historical event but a pivotal moment orchestrated by God.

At this juncture, it is essential to address a common misunderstanding concerning the nativity scene, particularly about the location of Jesus' birth. Some critics suggest that the Bible does not explicitly state Jesus was born in a stable. Although the text does not use those exact words, it clearly indicates that after His birth, Jesus was wrapped in cloths and placed in a manger, a fixture commonly found in places that house animals (Luke 2:7).

Considering the practical aspects of this detail offers clarity. It is highly unlikely that Mary, immediately after giving birth, would move her newborn any significant distance to lay him in a manger unless they were already in a setting where animals were kept. Logically, this suggests that the birth occurred in a stable, not elsewhere requiring relocation after the birth. The inclusion of a manger in the narrative is not merely a quaint detail but a poignant reminder of the humble circumstances surrounding Jesus' birth.

The argument that Jesus might have been born in a different location and then moved to a manger does not align with the narrative's straightforward depiction. Such a stance unnecessarily complicates what the Bible clearly aims to convey—the simplicity and humility of the event. The description of Jesus, wrapped in cloths and lying in a manger, inherently indicates His first moments were spent in the most humble of surroundings. This critical detail emphasizes the modest beginnings of one whose life and teachings would profoundly impact the world. It leads to a simple and logical conclusion: Jesus was born right there in the stable, making any debate on this point an unnecessary distraction from the powerful message of the Nativity.

Another frequent point of debate among skeptics and historians is whether the Roman census, as described in the Bible, actually occurred.

THE LIFE OF CHRIST JESUS

Some question the historical accuracy of the narrative, but a practical examination of the context provided in Scripture can offer a convincing case for the occurrence of this census.

Consider the detail mentioned in the Gospel of Luke: "there was no room in the inn" (Luke 2:7). This is not just a trivial detail; it provides a significant insight into the social conditions of the time. Mary, despite being on the verge of childbirth—a condition that typically evokes sympathy and triggers acts of kindness—could find no room for shelter. This suggests an unusually high volume of people in Bethlehem at that time.

Why would there be such an influx of travelers that not even a pregnant woman could find lodging? Under Roman rule, such a scenario is most plausibly explained by an event that would compel widespread travel, like a decree from the emperor. The most logical reason for such a decree would be a census, requiring individuals to return to their ancestral homes to be counted and taxed. This practice not only fits within the historical framework of Roman administrative control but also perfectly aligns with the Gospel narrative.

The total lack of available accommodations in Bethlehem, even for someone as vulnerable as Mary, strongly supports the existence of a census. It indicates that there was indeed a significant, government-mandated movement of populations returning to their ancestral homes, exactly as described in the biblical account. To dismiss the census is to overlook these practical implications that the narrative clearly presents. The logical conclusion, backed by the context of Roman governance and the specifics of the account, is that the census indeed took place, just as Luke describes.

God's grand plan did not just culminate with the birth of Jesus; it included what could be described as the most magnificent birthday celebration ever. He enlisted angels and celestial beings to herald this momentous occasion. These heavenly hosts filled the skies with joyful song, creating what would become the first Christmas choir, a spectacular display of celestial joy celebrating the arrival of Jesus, the Savior of the world.

The First Christmas Celebration

I initially thought of titling this chapter "Angels and Shepherds," but I chose "The First Christmas Celebration" instead to address a common misunderstanding. Some believe that Christmas celebrations were originally pagan customs incorporated into Christianity centuries after Christ's birth. However, the true origin of Christmas is deeply rooted in a moment of awe and wonder that occurred in a field just outside Bethlehem.

On a serene night, shepherds tending to their flocks became the first witnesses to the birth of Jesus Christ. The Bible describes this profound moment: Suddenly, an angel of the Lord appeared before them, and the glory of the Lord shone around them. Although they were initially terrified, the angel reassured them, saying, "Do not be afraid. I bring you good news that will cause great joy for all the people. Today in the town of David a Savior has been born to you; he is the Messiah, the Lord" (Luke 2:10-11).

The spectacle escalated as the sky filled with a multitude of heavenly hosts, all praising God and proclaiming, "Glory to God in the highest heaven, and on earth peace to those on whom his favor rests" (Luke 2:14). This chorus of angels, the first Christmas choir, heralded to the world that a miraculous event had occurred—one that would forever alter the course of human history.

The choice of shepherds as the recipients of this divine announcement is noteworthy. In those times, shepherds were often seen as lowly and insignificant. Yet, it was to these humble individuals that the angels appeared, highlighting God's tendency to uplift the humble and demonstrating that His salvation is accessible to everyone, not just the elite or powerful.

Compelled by the angels' message, the shepherds went to see the newborn Savior. They found Mary, Joseph, and the baby Jesus lying in the manger. After witnessing this, they shared what they had been told about this child, and all who heard their story were amazed (Luke 2:15-18).

Now, addressing the misconception that Christmas celebrations are of pagan origin and began centuries after Christ's birth, this narrative often proliferates through secular media and some liberal theologians. This portrayal is both inaccurate and a misunderstanding of scriptural events. The first Christmas celebration, as the scripture reveals, occurred on the very night of Jesus' birth, with angels and shepherds commemorating the event. The angelic choir that night shows that the celebration of Christ's birth began immediately, not centuries later.

The reason early Christians did not widely celebrate Christmas initially was not because of pagan influences but due to the life-threatening risks associated with being a Christian during periods of intense persecution. The situation shifted when Emperor Constantine converted to Christianity and legalized the religion throughout the Roman Empire, allowing Christians to celebrate openly without fear of persecution. Therefore, the Christmas celebration as we know it today is not a later adaptation of pagan practices but a revival of the original celebration of Christ's birth—a celebration marked by heavenly joy and divine proclamation, setting a precedent for future Christmas observances. This first celebration, featuring a celestial choir and humble shepherds, was truly the inaugural commemoration of the birth of Christ, filled with divine joy and celestial song.

The Presentation

Forty days after Jesus was born, an event took place that marked His first formal introduction to the religious community. In accordance with the Law of Moses and longstanding tradition, Mary and Joseph brought Jesus to the temple for His presentation. This act was a testament to their devout faith, as the Law required every firstborn son to be dedicated to the Lord, accompanied by a sacrificial offering (Leviticus 12). The Bible details this event in Luke, stating, "When the time came for the purification rites required by the Law of Moses, Joseph and Mary took him to Jerusalem to present him to the Lord" (Luke 2:22).

Upon entering the temple, Mary and Joseph experienced something extraordinary that transcended traditional rites. They met Simeon, a righteous and devout man who had received a divine promise that he would not die before seeing the Messiah. Guided by the Holy Spirit, Simeon came to the temple just as the couple arrived with Jesus. Holding Jesus in his arms, Simeon praised God, proclaiming, "Sovereign Lord, as you have promised, you may now dismiss your servant in peace. For my eyes have seen your salvation, which you have prepared in the sight of all nations: a light for revelation to the Gentiles, and the glory of your people Israel" (Luke 2:29-32).

This moment was profound as it signified the recognition of Jesus as the awaited Messiah by a devout follower, as foretold by divine revelation. Simeon also blessed them and delivered a powerful prophecy to Mary: "This child is destined to cause the falling and rising of many in Israel, and to be a sign that will be spoken against, so that the thoughts of many hearts will be revealed—and a sword will pierce your own soul too" (Luke 2:34-35). This prophecy outlined the significant impact Jesus' life would have and the deep personal pain Mary would endure as his mother.

Mary's role as the mother of Jesus was a journey filled with immense joy and profound sorrow, reflecting the ultimate expression of faith mixed with heartache. From the miraculous announcement of her divine pregnancy to the devastating scene at the cross, Mary was the only person to witness the full span of Jesus' earthly life, experiencing both the heights of His achievements and the depths of His suffering.

The presentation in the temple also brought them into contact with Anna, a prophetess who had dedicated many years to worship after becoming a widow. Upon seeing Jesus, Anna recognized Him as the Messiah and eagerly shared this revelation with all who awaited the redemption of Jerusalem. The Bible details her background: 'There was also a prophet, Anna, the daughter of Penuel, of the tribe of Asher. She was very old; she had lived with her husband seven years after her marriage, and then was a widow until she was eighty-four. She never left the temple but worshiped night and day, fasting and praying. Coming up to them at that very moment, she gave thanks to God and spoke about the child to all who were looking forward to the redemption of Jerusalem' (Luke 2:36-38).

Here, I must note a minor yet significant detail—the precise description of Anna as 'the daughter of Penuel, of the tribe of Asher.' This specific identification, including her tribal affiliation, underscores the accuracy of the biblical narrative, reinforcing its historical reliability.

This event was more than a mere religious observance; it was a pivotal moment confirming Jesus' identity as the Savior and fulfilling divine promises. The encounters with Simeon and Anna underscored the early recognition of Jesus' messianic role, affirming His purpose as foreseen by those devoted to God.

The Visit of the Magi

The visit of the Magi, often referred to as the Wise Men or Kings from the East, is one of the most captivating moments in the story of Jesus' birth. This event is more than just a story of a long journey guided by a starlit sky; it represents a profound acknowledgment of Jesus' kingship and divine mission from beyond the borders of Judea, highlighting the universal significance of His arrival.

The Bible details this extraordinary visit in the book of Matthew, describing how these Magi from the east reached Jerusalem after Jesus' birth. "After Jesus was born in Bethlehem in Judea, during the time of King Herod, Magi from the east came to Jerusalem and asked, 'Where is the one who has been born King of the Jews? We saw his star when it rose and have come to worship him'" (Matthew 2:1-2). The Magi, likely astronomers or astrologers, interpreted the appearance of a new star as a sign heralding the birth of a significant king and set out to find and honor Him.

Their journey was lengthy and arduous, indicating the magnitude of their mission. Upon reaching Jerusalem, their inquiries about the "newborn King of the Jews" disturbed King Herod and the city's inhabitants. Threatened by the prophecy of a new king, Herod deceitfully asked the Magi to inform him of the child's whereabouts under the pretense of also wanting to worship the child.

Following the star to Bethlehem, the Magi finally found Jesus with His mother, Mary. Their reaction to finally reaching their destination is beautifully captured: "When they saw the star, they were overjoyed. On coming to the house, they saw the child with his mother Mary, and they bowed down and worshiped him. Then they opened their treasures and presented him with gifts of gold, frankincense, and myrrh" (Matthew 2:10-11). The gifts they brought were rich with symbolism: gold recognizing Jesus' royalty, frankincense His divinity, and myrrh, used in embalming, hinting at His destined sacrifice.

Forewarned in a dream not to return to Herod, the Magi took a different route home, evading Herod's malicious intent. This precautionary move shows the depth of their wisdom and their crucial role in safeguarding the newborn king. Herod's subsequent fury and the impending danger forced Joseph and Mary to flee to Egypt with Jesus, ensuring His safety from the king's murderous decree.

The Flight to Egypt

When King Herod realized that the Magi had not returned to him as he had commanded, his fear of losing his throne to the newborn "King of the Jews"—as referred to by the Magi—drove him to commit a horrifying act. Herod ordered the massacre of all boys in Bethlehem and its vicinity who were two years old and under. This brutal command was based on the timing of the star's appearance, as relayed by the Magi. This massacre was a dark moment in history, driven by jealousy and the fear of losing power, and serves as a stark reminder of how deep human sinfulness can go, especially in the quest for control.

This appalling event underscores the contrast between the kingdom of God, which Jesus came to establish, and the kingdoms of this world, which are often built on violence, fear, and oppression. Jesus entered a world where the innocent suffered at the hands of the powerful—a world far removed from safety and peace.

To protect Jesus from Herod's violent decree, Joseph was divinely warned in a dream. The Gospel of Matthew recounts this urgent directive: "When they [the Magi] had gone, an angel of the Lord appeared to Joseph in a dream. 'Get up,' he said, 'take the child and his mother and escape to Egypt. Stay there until I tell you, for Herod is going to search for the child to kill him.' So he got up, took the child and his mother during the night and left for Egypt" (Matthew 2:13-14).

Joseph's immediate and obedient response to God's warning is a recurring theme throughout his involvement in the Gospel narratives. His action was not just a simple escape; it was laden with symbolism. Historically, Egypt had been a place of both refuge and bondage for the Israelites. Now, it served as a sanctuary for the Messiah, echoing the profound connections between past deliverances and the present protection of Jesus.

The Flight to Egypt emphasizes the vulnerability and humanity of Jesus. Despite being the Son of God, He was not immune to persecution. This facet of the narrative deeply aligns with Christian teachings about the Incarnation—God taking on human form and fully experiencing the human condition, including its adversities. The journey to Egypt and the eventual return after Herod's death, which we will discuss next, represent the enduring hope and the ultimate victory of God's plan over human machinations. Through these trials, the narrative reassures believers of the steadfast presence and providence of God, even in the face of great threats.

Return to Nazareth from Egypt

The return of Mary, Joseph, and the young Jesus to Nazareth from Egypt marks a crucial chapter in the early life of the one who would become the Savior of the world. After escaping King Herod's wrath and living temporarily in Egypt, they were divinely instructed that it was safe to return to their homeland. This journey back not only symbolized a return to normal life but also fulfilled several ancient prophecies concerning the Messiah.

The Bible details in the book of Matthew how it became safe for the family to leave Egypt: "After Herod died, an angel of the Lord appeared in a dream to Joseph in Egypt and said, 'Get up, take the child and his mother and go to the land of Israel, for those who were trying to take the child's life are dead'" (Matthew 2:19-20). This divine message prompted Joseph to bring his family back to Israel, setting the stage for the next developments in God's redemptive plan.

However, their return was fraught with challenges. Learning that Archelaus was reigning in Judea in place of his father Herod, Joseph was apprehensive about returning there. Following another divine warning in a dream, he opted instead for the district of Galilee, settling in the town of Nazareth (Matthew 2:22-23). It was in Nazareth that Jesus would grow "in wisdom and stature, and in favor with God and man" (Luke 2:52).

Moreover, this relocation was prophetically significant. It fulfilled the prophecy from Hosea 11:1, "Out of Egypt I called my son." While this initially referred to the nation of Israel, Matthew interprets it messianically, applying it to Jesus' return from Egypt. The decision to reside in Nazareth also aligned with the prophecy that the Messiah would be called a Nazarene—a reflection not of a specific scriptural verse but an understanding that the Messiah would emerge from humble and lowly origins. Nazareth, a town often regarded with disdain, as echoed in Nathanael's skeptical remark in the Gospel of John, "Nazareth! Can anything good come from there?" (John 1:46), underscores this humility.

Settling in Nazareth, a place of little political importance, likely contributed to the obscurity that marked Jesus' early years, preserving Him from undue attention until His public ministry began. This period of relative anonymity lasted until Jesus was about thirty years old, emerging publicly to be baptized by John the Baptist.

As we move forward, we will explore more about His childhood, the so-called silent years, and the significant yet formative stages of His life that prepared Him for His ministry and mission.

THE SILENT YEARS

This section covers the following topics:

- *Introduction*
- *The Boy in the Temple*
- *The First Phase of Silent Years*
- *Mary and Joseph's Parenting*
- *The Carpenter's Son*
- *Was Jesus Married?*
- *The Brothers of Jesus*

CHRIS MORAIS

Introduction

The life of Jesus, as documented in the Bible, includes a significant span often referred to as 'The Silent Years.' These years, largely unrecorded in the Scriptures, encompass two key phases of Jesus' life. The first silent period spans from His early childhood after returning to Nazareth until He is twelve years old, culminating in a memorable event at the Temple. This episode, which marks His first recorded interaction in Scripture since infancy, showcases His profound understanding of the scriptures and a clear sense of His divine mission.

Following this event, there is another prolonged silent period extending from age twelve until the beginning of His public ministry at about age thirty. While the Bible offers little detail about these years, insights can be drawn from the Temple incident and community references to Him as the carpenter's son, allowing for thoughtful speculation about His formative years.

Drawing on Jesus' interaction at the Temple at age 12 and public perception of Him as the 'carpenter's son', this section offers speculative insights into what might have transpired during these unrecorded years. Additionally, the incident where Jesus briefly goes missing during a festival has prompted critics to question the parenting style of Mary and Joseph. This topic is addressed here.

Furthermore, this section tackles the perennial question of whether Jesus was married. The conclusion drawn here is that such speculations are unfounded sensationalism; there is no biblical evidence to support that Jesus was married.

Lastly, the section would not be complete without discussing who Jesus' brothers were. Contrary to some beliefs, they were neither Mary and Joseph's children nor Joseph's children from a previous marriage. They were more likely His cousins or distant relatives. This interpretation is also explored logically.

Let us dive deeper into these intriguing aspects of Jesus' life.

The Boy in the Temple

The account of the Boy Jesus in the Temple stands out as the sole story of His childhood in the scriptures, offering a rare glimpse into His early development and hinting at His destined path. This narrative unfolds during a family pilgrimage to Jerusalem for the Passover Festival, a significant observance for the Jewish community. After the festival, Mary and Joseph began their journey back to Nazareth, unknowingly leaving Jesus behind in Jerusalem. Believing He was with their travel group, they traveled for a day before realizing He was missing. The anxiety and urgency they felt upon this discovery led them to hurry back to Jerusalem in search of Him.

Three days later, they found Jesus in the temple courts, engaging with the teachers, listening intently, and asking insightful questions. Those who heard Him were astounded at His understanding and responses (Luke 2:46-47). This episode is notable for several reasons. It not only showcases Jesus' profound grasp of religious and scriptural knowledge at a young age but also highlights His capacity to discuss complex religious topics, leaving even seasoned scholars impressed.

Upon finding Him, His parents' astonishment was evident. Mary expressed her distress, saying, "Son, why have you treated us like this? Your father and I have been anxiously searching for you" (Luke 2:48). Jesus' reply to His mother is telling and significant: "Why were you searching for me? Didn't you know I had to be in my Father's house?" (Luke 2:49). This response underscores Jesus' awareness of His unique relationship with God, even as a child. His words were not a mark of disobedience or disregard for His earthly parents; rather, they reflected His deep commitment to His divine purpose. To put it in contemporary terms, it is akin to someone at work reassuring their spouse over the phone that they are where they must be—fulfilling their responsibilities.

This chapter sets the stage to further explore how these early experiences and silent years shaped the profound teachings and path of Jesus, which I will continue to elaborate on in the following sections.

The First Phase of Silent Years

From the account of Jesus in the temple at age twelve, we gain valuable insights into His early life and spiritual development. It is clear that Jesus was endowed with a remarkable wisdom from a young age, a gift that undoubtedly came from God. The scriptures, likely a fundamental part of His upbringing both at home and in local synagogues, were not merely memorized by Him but profoundly understood. This deep comprehension is vividly showcased when Jesus, still a child, confidently engages in discussions with well-educated religious leaders. His ability to debate these seasoned scholars, despite His young age, underscores His exceptional grasp of scripture and points to His unique nature and divine mission.

Additionally, Jesus' behavior in the temple reveals an extraordinary self-awareness of His identity and purpose. When His parents confronted Him about why He stayed behind in Jerusalem, Jesus responded with a significant question: "Didn't you know I had to be in my Father's house?" (Luke 2:49). This response reflects a deep understanding of His relationship with God the Father, indicating that He saw Himself as more than just the son of Mary and Joseph. This early expression of His identity as the Son of God suggests that even as a child, Jesus was fully aware of His divine role, highlighting that His life was destined to follow a heavenly ordained path.

Furthermore, Jesus' choice to remain in the temple and engage with the teachers of the law was not an act of disobedience towards His earthly parents but a manifestation of His commitment to His divine mission. By choosing to discuss the scriptures instead of immediately returning home with His parents, Jesus demonstrated where His ultimate responsibilities lay. This action was not about rebellion; it was about affirming His dedication to the mission He was sent to fulfill. His presence in the temple, a place of learning and spiritual growth, engaging positively with His religious heritage, was a clear indicator that His actions were driven not by youthful defiance but by a deep commitment to fulfill His calling.

These moments in the temple were not just a display of precociousness; they were a declaration of His preparedness and eagerness to undertake the responsibilities of His ministry. Jesus' time in the temple, therefore, is not just a footnote in His life story but a profound prelude to His public ministry, illustrating from a young age His deep connection with His divine purpose and His readiness to embrace His role as the Messiah.

Mary and Joseph's Parenting

The episode where Mary and Joseph temporarily lost track of Jesus during their visit to Jerusalem raises questions about their attentiveness as parents. However, labeling this incident as negligence misunderstands the cultural norms of the time and overlooks the practices still found in many traditional societies today. In the community where Jesus grew up, the approach to child-rearing was collective. This setting, where "it takes a village to raise a child," allowed parents like Mary and Joseph to feel secure knowing their son was in the care of trusted friends and family during the bustling festival in Jerusalem.

Additionally, it was customary for children, especially those nearing adolescence, to be granted certain freedoms to explore their social and religious environments. This cultural practice, still observed in many communities around the world today, fosters independence within the safety of a familiar environment, overseen informally by the entire community.

It is also crucial to remember the profound dedication and courage Mary and Joseph exhibited from the very beginning. From risking their lives to save Jesus from King Herod's murderous decree to their escape to Egypt, their actions consistently demonstrated their commitment and love for their child. The momentary lapse in tracking Jesus' location does not indicate a lack of care but reflects an anomaly in a chaotic, festive setting, where they believed in the safety provided by their community.

When Mary and Joseph found Jesus, He was in the temple, engaged safely and constructively with scholars, not in a place of danger but in an environment that fostered His growth. This scenario underscores that Jesus was not only in a safe place but also in a setting that encouraged Him to articulate His thoughts and debate theological matters—an extraordinary level of freedom for a child of that era and even by today's standards.

This environment illustrates the nurturing aspect of His upbringing, which afforded Him the intellectual and spiritual freedom to explore and express His unique insights. Moreover, it highlights the preparation He received for His future role, which went beyond ordinary parenting. Mary and Joseph's actions here should not be viewed as negligent but as a manifestation of their profound trust in their child's extraordinary destiny and abilities, demonstrating their deep understanding of His divine nature and mission.

As we continue, will delve into the second phase of the silent years, focusing on how Jesus came to be known as the carpenter's son and what this implies about His life and development during this period.

The Carpenter's Son

The second phase of the Silent Years unfolds after Jesus' significant interaction with the temple teachers at age twelve. Following this event, the Bible recounts His return to Nazareth, noting, "Then he went down to Nazareth with them and was obedient to them. But his mother treasured all these things in her heart. And Jesus grew in wisdom and stature, and in favor with God and man" (Luke 2:51-52). Despite the silence in the scriptures about the subsequent years until the start of His public ministry, references to Jesus as the carpenter's son provide some speculative insight into this period.

The Gospel of Matthew captures the community's perception during His ministry: "Isn't this the carpenter's son? Isn't his mother's name Mary, and aren't his brothers James, Joseph, Simon, and Judas?" (Matthew 13:55). This portrayal suggests that Jesus was primarily known through His family and occupational ties, embedding Him deeply in the everyday life of a typical Galilean village.

It is important to clarify that the Bible does not explicitly state that Jesus was a carpenter, only that He was the "son of a carpenter." Based on this and the customary practices of the time, it is likely that Jesus would have learned and perhaps practiced carpentry alongside His earthly father, Joseph. This apprenticeship would have equipped Jesus not only with practical skills but also with profound insights into the lives and experiences of ordinary people. As a carpenter, Jesus would have interacted with a broad spectrum of individuals, from the humblest families to the more affluent, giving Him a unique perspective on human nature and relationships.

His experiences during these silent years evidently informed His teachings, which are rich with references and metaphors drawn from daily life. The wisdom and understanding that Jesus displayed in the temple at twelve would have continued to develop as He balanced work, study, and prayer. This ongoing growth is evident when He commenced His public ministry by reading from the book of Isaiah in the synagogue (Luke 4:16-21), demonstrating a deep understanding of Scripture that had been honed over years of silent preparation.

Furthermore, another testament to His engagement with the Scriptures during these silent years is the episode of His temptation in the wilderness. Here, when faced with the devil's cunning temptations, Jesus countered each challenge with scripture, consistently responding, "It is written..." This suggests that His silent years were not only spent in labor but in diligent study of the Scriptures, preparing for the challenges of His ministry.

In conclusion, the Silent Years of Jesus, marked by His work as a carpenter and His continuous study of the Scriptures, shed light on His preparation for public ministry. This period underscores the dignity of manual labor, the importance of scriptural study, and the sanctity of ordinary life, all of which profoundly influenced His approach to ministry. Jesus' life during these years exemplifies the holistic nature of spiritual growth, where daily work and scriptural meditation intertwine to deepen one's understanding of God and His purposes.

Was Jesus Married?

A controversial topic that often emerges regarding the Silent Years is whether Jesus was married. Claims about Jesus being married typically stem from dubious interpretations of both canonical and Gnostic gospels. It is crucial to state clearly that these claims are not grounded in truth but are the product of misinformation and misinterpretation. Unfortunately, some leverage these unfounded theories to stir controversy for personal gain. Disappointingly, even some academics—who should uphold intellectual integrity—propagate these myths, often driven by the lure of sensationalism or commercial motives. Let us approach the question of Jesus being married with logic and critical examination, as truth is inherently logical.

In the culture in which Jesus lived, marriage was not only acceptable but also esteemed. The Bible clearly shows that Jesus' disciple Peter was married, as evidenced by Jesus healing Peter's mother-in-law (Matthew 8:14-15). However, the permissibility of an act does not mandate its practice. While Jesus had the freedom to marry, the absence of any mention of a wife in the Gospels strongly suggests that He did not marry.

Jesus' mission transcended ordinary human experiences; He was divinely appointed for the salvation of humanity. His path was to end in crucifixion and resurrection, a sacrifice for the sins of the world (John 3:16-17). His mission was to establish a new covenant, not to seek matrimonial ties, which could have distracted from and complicated His divine purpose. Thus, Jesus likely chose a life of celibacy, dedicated entirely to His spiritual mission.

Consider the wedding at Cana, where Jesus performed His first miracle (John 2:1-11). If Jesus had been married, customary norms of the time would have placed His wife by His side during such an event. Furthermore, accounts of Jesus' family visiting Him mention His mother and brothers but not a wife (Mark 3:31-35), pointing again to His likely celibacy.

Perhaps the most telling evidence comes from Jesus' final moments on the cross. He entrusted the care of His mother to His beloved disciple John (John 19:26-27). If Jesus had a wife, it stands to reason that He would have made provisions for her as well, yet there is no mention of a wife in any of these critical narratives.

Mary Magdalene has often been at the center of much speculation and controversy, but it is clear from biblical texts that she was not the wife of Jesus. Rather, she was a devout follower who experienced a profound transformation under His ministry. According to the Bible, Jesus cast out seven demons from her, an act of deliverance that led her to dedicate her life to following Him (Luke 8:2). Her gratitude and reverence for Jesus were evident, as she supported His ministry and was present during some of the most pivotal moments in His life.

Mary Magdalene's role extended beyond just a follower; she was present at the crucifixion, observed where Jesus was laid to rest, and importantly, she was the first to witness the empty tomb. Her encounter with the risen Christ is particularly telling. When Jesus appeared to her, she addressed Him as "Rabbi" (John 20:16), which means teacher. This term of respect highlights her relationship with Jesus—she saw Him as her teacher and spiritual leader, not a spouse.

The portrayal of Mary Magdalene calling Jesus "Rabbi" underscores the inaccuracy of claims that she was his wife. It reflects a relationship based on spiritual leadership and discipleship, aligning with the broader New Testament narrative that does not support any claims of Jesus being married. Mary Magdalene's story is one of loyalty, transformation, and pivotal witness to Jesus's resurrection, emphasizing her significant role in the Christian faith as a leading woman disciple, not a hidden spouse.

Thus, the theory that Jesus was married lacks empirical support and is built on conjecture, often promoted by those with vested interests. The Gospels, our most reliable sources about Jesus' life, depict Him as a figure wholly dedicated to His divine mission, without any distractions that a marital relationship would entail. Thus, we should be wary of sensational claims that lack basis in fact, prioritizing the pursuit of truth and the integrity of scriptural evidence.

The Brothers of Jesus

A discussion of "The Silent Years" of Jesus' life would not be complete without addressing the identities of His brothers—James, Joseph, Simon, and Judas—as mentioned in Matthew 13:55 during the narrative of the 'Carpenter's Son'. The prevailing narrative posits that these individuals were either the children of Mary and Joseph born after Jesus or the children from a previous marriage of Joseph. However, both assumptions are unlikely when examined in the light of scripture and logical reasoning.

First, let us consider their mission and presence at critical moments in Jesus' life. Joseph and Mary were divinely chosen to nurture and protect Jesus, the Messiah. Given this monumental responsibility, it is logical to presume that their lives were wholly dedicated to this mission. At the crucifixion, a profoundly significant event, none of the so-called brothers were mentioned as present to support their mother or to stand by Jesus. In typical familial settings, especially during times of crisis, one would expect at least one sibling to be present. Their absence strongly suggests that these individuals were not Mary's biological children, nor were they Joseph's offspring from a previous union.

Moreover, the assumption that Joseph had other children before marrying Mary and abandoned them to protect Jesus and Mary contradicts what we know of his character. Joseph is described in the scriptures as a righteous man, deeply committed to protecting Mary's dignity upon discovering her pregnancy. Such a man, portrayed consistently as honorable and righteous, is unlikely to neglect his parental duties towards other children.

THE LIFE OF CHRIST JESUS

Another compelling piece of evidence comes from the account of Jesus at the temple at age twelve. This episode makes no mention of other siblings joining the journey to Jerusalem, which would be an unusual omission if Jesus had younger brothers at that time. If Mary and Joseph did not have any other children for at least twelve years following Jesus' birth, the sudden appearance of four sons afterward seems highly improbable.

Therefore, who were these individuals referred to as Jesus' brothers? A plausible explanation, common in many cultures both historically and presently, is that the term "brothers" could refer to cousins or close relatives. In many Middle Eastern, Asian, and even contemporary multicultural societies, it is customary to refer to cousins and other close relatives as brothers or sisters. This familial language extends beyond biological connections, emphasizing close bonds and relationships within extended families.

Thus, the most reasonable conclusion is that James, Joseph, Simon, and Judas were likely Jesus' cousins or close family relatives, not His direct siblings. This interpretation aligns with cultural practices and resolves the contradictions that arise from viewing them as His immediate family.

BREAKING THE SILENCE

This section covers the following topics:

- *Introduction*
- *The Voice Prepares the Way*
- *The Baptism*
- *The Temptation*

Introduction

After years of quiet growth and preparation, the moment arrived to break the silence. This new chapter in the biblical narrative begins with a key prophetic figure who connects Old Testament prophecies with their New Testament fulfillment: John the Baptist.

John the Baptist stepped onto the scene in the wilderness, calling for repentance as he preached a baptism of repentance for the forgiveness of sins. His robust, prophetic demeanor and his message directly fulfilled the prophecy from Isaiah about a voice crying out in the wilderness, urging people to prepare the way for the Lord (Isaiah 40:3).

Following the groundwork laid by John, Jesus initiated His public ministry with His baptism in the Jordan River. This event was more than a mere ritual; it was a profound affirmation of Jesus' identity and mission. As Jesus emerged from the water, the heavens opened—a divine endorsement of His sonship—as the Spirit descended like a dove and a voice from heaven declared, "This is my beloved Son, with whom I am well pleased" (Matthew 3:16-17). This heavenly proclamation at His baptism not only confirmed Jesus' divine nature but also publicly endorsed His acceptance of His messianic mission.

Immediately following His baptism, Jesus was led by the Spirit into the wilderness. There, He fasted for forty days and faced temptations from Satan. This period was not just a test of physical endurance but a demonstration of Jesus' spiritual fortitude and His mastery over worldly temptations. In stark contrast to Adam, who yielded to temptation in the lush Garden of Eden, Jesus resisted temptation in the harsh wilderness, thereby overturning humanity's past failures and setting a new standard for obedience and trust in God. Each challenge during this time not only prepared Jesus for the trials of His ministry but also underscored His deep scriptural insight and commitment to righteousness.

The events of John the Baptist's clarion call, Jesus' baptism, and His triumph over the temptations in the wilderness collectively signal the vigorous onset of Jesus' ministry. These episodes fulfill multiple Old Testament prophecies and lay a robust theological groundwork for His subsequent teachings, miracles, and the ultimate sacrifice He would offer for humanity.

The Voice Prepares the Way

Before Jesus began His public ministry, a compelling figure named John the Baptist emerged in the wilderness. Clad in camel's hair and surviving on locusts and wild honey, John was not just a rustic hermit but a fiery preacher with a mission: to prepare the way for the Lord. His role was prophesied by Isaiah: "A voice of one calling in the wilderness, 'Prepare the way for the Lord, make straight paths for him'" (Isaiah 40:3). John's calling was to spark a spiritual awakening, urging people to return to God in anticipation of the Messiah's arrival.

The Gospels of Matthew, Mark, Luke, and John all underscore John the Baptist's critical role in the narrative of Jesus' ministry. Mark starts by linking John to the prophecies of Isaiah and Malachi: "As it is written in Isaiah the prophet: 'I will send my messenger ahead of you, who will prepare your way'— 'a voice of one calling in the wilderness, 'Prepare the way for the Lord, make straight paths for him'" (Mark 1:2-3). John's message was straightforward and powerful: "Repent, for the kingdom of heaven has come near" (Matthew 3:2).

John did not just preach; he acted. He baptized people in the Jordan River as a symbol of their repentance and new life dedicated to God. This act was not merely ceremonial but a profound declaration of readiness to receive the Messiah. John's baptisms drew large crowds from Jerusalem, Judea, and the surrounding regions, with people from diverse backgrounds coming forward to confess their sins and be baptized.

John the Baptist is also pivotal in affirming the messianic identity of Jesus. His recognition of Jesus as "the Lamb of God, who takes away the sin of the world" (John 1:29), and his fulfillment of Old Testament prophecies, bolster the continuity and authenticity of the biblical narrative. John's ministry reached a climax when he baptized Jesus in the Jordan River, marking the official start of Jesus' ministry, despite John's own feelings of unworthiness to perform the baptism.

However, John's ministry faced challenges, particularly from the religious elite. When Pharisees and Sadducees appeared at one of his baptisms, John did not hesitate to confront their hypocrisy, branding them a "brood of vipers" and urging them to show genuine repentance (Matthew 3:7-8). His fearless proclamation of the truth, regardless of the audience, emphasized the critical nature of his mission and the urgent need for true change.

John the Baptist's life and work exemplify humility, dedication, and the crucial role of preparing the way for Jesus. He understood that his purpose was to direct others to Christ, famously stating, "He must become greater; I must become less" (John 3:30). This mindset of selfless dedication serves as a model for all believers, reminding us of the importance of living lives that not only anticipate but actively make way for Jesus in our hearts and in the world.

The Baptism

The Gospels recount an important moment when Jesus traveled from Galilee to the Jordan River to be baptized by John the Baptist. Upon Jesus' arrival, John was initially reluctant to perform the baptism. He recognized Jesus as sinless and understood the magnitude of His divine mission, saying, "I need to be baptized by you, and do you come to me?" (Matthew 3:14). Despite John's reservations, Jesus insisted on being baptized, stating it was necessary to "fulfill all righteousness." This act illustrated Jesus' unwavering dedication to fulfilling God's will in every facet of His life.

As Jesus was baptized and rose from the waters, an extraordinary event unfolded. The heavens opened, and the Spirit of God descended upon Him like a dove, marking a visually and spiritually transformative moment that underscored the Holy Spirit's empowerment for the ministry Jesus was about to undertake. Simultaneously, a voice from heaven proclaimed, "This is my Son, whom I love; with him I am well pleased" (Matthew 3:17). This divine affirmation not only revealed Jesus' identity as the beloved Son of God but also publicly endorsed His mission to redeem humanity.

The baptism of Jesus carries profound significance on multiple levels. Firstly, it demonstrates Jesus' solidarity with humanity's plight and His commitment to redeeming it. Although sinless, Jesus chose to be baptized, symbolically aligning Himself with the sinful nature of humankind that He came to save.

Secondly, this event publicly confirmed His divine sonship. The heavenly voice affirming, "This is my Son, whom I love; with him I am well pleased," marked the official beginning of His public ministry, validated by divine approval.

Thirdly, the baptism represents a clear manifestation of the Trinity, one of the core elements of Christian doctrine. The presence of the Father (voice from heaven), the Son (Jesus being baptized), and the Holy Spirit (descending like a dove) beautifully illustrates the triune nature of God, highlighting the unity and distinct roles within the Godhead.

Thus, the baptism of Jesus stands not just as a historical account but as a foundational event that illuminates His divine nature, His mission of salvation, and His exemplary obedience to God's will. It serves as a powerful testament to the start of His transformative ministry on earth.

The Temptation

After His baptism by John the Baptist, Jesus was led by the Spirit into the wilderness. There, He fasted for forty days and nights, entering a state of physical weakness but spiritual alertness. It was in this challenging setting that Jesus faced one of His greatest tests: the temptations by the devil. The narratives of these temptations in the Gospels not only underscore Jesus' humanity in facing temptation but also His divinity in conquering it.

The first temptation centered on a direct appeal to Jesus' physical hunger. The devil challenged Jesus to turn stones into bread, to which Jesus, despite His hunger, responded with a powerful scripture from Deuteronomy 8:3: "Man shall not live on bread alone, but on every word that comes from the mouth of God" (Matthew 4:4). This reply underscores a profound truth: life is sustained not merely by physical nourishment but by the spiritual sustenance of God's Word.

In the second temptation, Jesus was taken to the highest point of the temple in Jerusalem. Here, the devil prodded Him to throw Himself down, misquoting scripture to suggest that angels would save Him. To this, Jesus responded with another scripture from Deuteronomy 6:16, "Do not put the Lord your God to the test" (Matthew 4:7). This moment targeted the nature of trust between God and humanity, advocating a demonstration of faith as a spectacle rather than as a genuine trust. Jesus' response reinforced the importance of a faith that does not demand miraculous signs but is rooted firmly in God's promises.

The third and final temptation involved the devil showing Jesus all the kingdoms of the world, offering Him earthly power and glory in exchange for worship. Jesus' answer was immediate and resolute, "Away from me, Satan! For it is written: 'Worship the Lord your God, and serve him only'" (Matthew 4:10), referencing Deuteronomy 6:13. This temptation aimed to divert Jesus from His divine mission by appealing to worldly authority, but Jesus' allegiance to His Father's plan remained steadfast.

Throughout each temptation, Jesus countered not with His own might or wisdom but with the authority of Scripture. This teaches us the power and importance of God's Word in resisting temptation. The devil attempted to twist scripture for his own purposes, a manipulation we still see today. Conversely, Jesus demonstrated the correct use of scripture: understood and applied appropriately within context.

The ordeal in the wilderness also equipped Jesus for His impending public ministry, showing His complete dependence on the Father and adherence to the Holy Spirit's guidance. It proclaimed that His kingdom was not anchored in this world and that His power derived not from earthly compromises but from His obedience to God. This episode is a critical demonstration of Jesus' mission and His preparation for the trials and triumphs that lay ahead in His journey to redeem humanity.

THE PUBLIC MINISTRY

———

This section covers the following topics:

- *Introduction*
- *The Chosen Twelve*
- *The Sermon on the Mount*
- *The Teachings*
- *Redefining the Law*
- *Teaching to Pray*
- *The Miracles*
- *The Parables*
- *The Transfiguration*
- *The Triumphal Entry*

CHRIS MORAIS

Introduction

The commencement of Jesus' public ministry marked a pivotal moment in history when the long-awaited Messiah emerged publicly to fulfill ancient prophecies and bring hope to a world in anticipation. Following His baptism by John the Baptist and His victorious encounter with temptation in the wilderness, Jesus, now filled with the Holy Spirit, returned to Galilee to start His divine mission of teaching, healing, and spreading the good news of God's kingdom.

The Gospel of Matthew recounts that Jesus initiated His ministry by moving from Nazareth to Capernaum, a move that fulfilled Isaiah's prophecy of a light shining upon those living in darkness in the regions of Zebulun and Naphtali (Matthew 4:13-16). This strategic shift not only placed Jesus in a more influential location but also signified the dawn of the promised redemption.

Jesus commenced His ministry with a definitive declaration of His mission. Central to Jesus' ministry was His call for repentance: "Repent, for the kingdom of heaven has come near" (Matthew 4:17), echoing and expanding upon John the Baptist's message with the Messiah's authority. More than a call for moral reform, Jesus' message invited people to a transformative relationship with God, characterized by grace, forgiveness, and the promise of eternal life.

A pivotal moment in Jesus' ministry was the selection of the Twelve Apostles. These men, from diverse backgrounds, were chosen not merely as followers but as emissaries of Jesus' teachings across the globe. The diversity and ordinariness of the Twelve highlight Jesus' message that God's kingdom welcomes everyone who responds to His call, regardless of their history or social standing. This strategic selection was part of Jesus' meticulous plan to ensure the perpetuation of His teachings beyond His time on Earth.

Accompanied by His disciples, Jesus traversed Galilee, teaching in synagogues, proclaiming the kingdom's good news. Unlike the day's religious authorities, Jesus taught with a unique authority that resonated deeply with His listeners.

Among His many instructions, the Sermon on the Mount is particularly significant, offering a radical reinterpretation of the Law. In this sermon, Jesus discusses the beatitudes, and principles of love, forgiveness, and the essence of the law—emphasizing inner righteousness over external rituals. This sermon not only raised the moral expectations of His followers but also assured blessings for those earnestly seeking to fulfill God's commands.

Jesus' ministry was also remarkable for its miracles, which confirmed His divine nature and compassion. Whether healing the ill, feeding thousands, calming storms, or raising the dead, these acts validated His divine identity, fulfilled Old Testament prophecies, and displayed His mercy. Each miracle was a testament that the kingdom of God was manifesting powerfully through His deeds. The miracles He performed—such as restoring sight to the blind, healing the lame, cleansing lepers, and expelling demons—affirmed His dominion over both physical and spiritual realms and solidified His identity as the Son of God.

Parables were another method Jesus used to impart spiritual truths. These simple yet profound stories challenged prevailing wisdom and opened up deeper spiritual insights to those willing to learn. Through parables, Jesus made complex divine realities accessible to all, inviting His audience to engage more deeply with spiritual truths.

THE LIFE OF CHRIST JESUS

The impact of Jesus' ministry was immediate and far-reaching. News of His works spread throughout Syria, compelling people to bring the sick and afflicted to Him, all of whom He healed (Matthew 4:24). Crowds gathered from all over, including Galilee, the Decapolis, Jerusalem, Judea, and beyond the Jordan, drawn by His hopeful message and compassionate deeds.

The Transfiguration of Jesus stands as another cornerstone event, revealing His divine glory to Peter, James, and John. This brief glimpse of His divine nature not only confirmed His divine sonship and the prophetic declarations about Him but also strengthened His disciples' faith as He approached His crucifixion.

Lastly, Jesus' Triumphal Entry into Jerusalem marked Him publicly as the messianic king. Fulfilling Zechariah's prophecy by riding on a donkey, He was celebrated by crowds hailing Him as the son of David. This event not only acknowledged His kingship but also set the stage for the climactic conclusion of His earthly mission—the passion and resurrection.

Through His teachings, miracles, and interactions, Jesus not only demonstrated God's love but also laid the groundwork for the gospel's spread, the church's establishment, and the enduring hope of salvation for all believers.

The Chosen Twelve

At the onset of His public ministry, Jesus made a strategic decision that would profoundly shape the future of Christianity. He selected twelve men from diverse walks of life to be His disciples. These men were not scholars or religious leaders but ordinary individuals, including fishermen, a tax collector, and a zealot. This selection underscored Jesus' message that the kingdom of God was accessible to everyone, not merely a privileged few.

Jesus' call to Peter and Andrew is one of the first recorded in the Gospels. These two brothers were fishermen by trade. As Jesus walked along the Sea of Galilee, He saw Simon Peter and Andrew casting a net into the lake. He called out to them, "Come, follow me, and I will send you out to fish for people." Immediately, they left their nets and followed Him (Matthew 4:18-20).

Right after calling Peter and Andrew, Jesus encountered another pair of brothers, James and John, the sons of Zebedee. They were in a boat with their father, preparing their nets. Jesus called them, and without hesitation, they left the boat and their father to follow Him (Matthew 4:21-22).

Matthew, also known as Levi, was a tax collector, a profession often despised by the Jewish people for its association with Roman oppression and corruption. Jesus saw Matthew sitting at the tax collector's booth and said to him, "Follow me." Matthew got up, left everything, and followed Jesus (Matthew 9:9).

Philip was from Bethsaida, the same town as Peter and Andrew. When Jesus found Philip, He said, "Follow me." Philip immediately accepted the call and later brought Nathanael to Jesus, saying, "We have found the one Moses wrote about in the Law, and about whom the prophets also wrote—Jesus of Nazareth, the son of Joseph" (John 1:43-45).

Philip found Nathanael (Bartholomew) and told him about Jesus. Skeptical at first, Nathanael asked, "Nazareth! Can anything good come from there?" Philip urged him to come and see. When Jesus saw Nathanael approaching, He said, "Here truly is an Israelite in whom there is no deceit." Nathanael was amazed that Jesus knew him and declared, "Rabbi, you are the Son of God; you are the king of Israel" (John 1:46-49).

Thomas, also known as Didymus, was called to be one of Jesus' disciples. Although the specific details of his initial calling are not provided in the Gospels, he is known for his skepticism and later profound declaration of faith when he saw the resurrected Jesus, exclaiming, "My Lord and my God!" (John 20:28).

James, the son of Alphaeus, often referred to as James the Lesser to distinguish him from James the son of Zebedee, was chosen by Jesus to be one of the twelve disciples. The details of his calling are not specified in the Gospels, but his inclusion among the twelve signifies his importance in Jesus' ministry (Matthew 10:3).

Simon, called the Zealot, was known for his fervent nationalism and desire for Jewish independence. He was chosen by Jesus to be one of the twelve disciples, representing the diverse backgrounds and perspectives among Jesus' followers (Matthew 10:4).

Thaddeus, also known as Judas son of James, is listed among the twelve disciples. Like several other disciples, the specifics of his calling are not detailed in the Gospels, but he played a vital role in Jesus' ministry (Luke 6:16).

Judas Iscariot, who would later betray Jesus, was also called to be one of the twelve disciples. His calling is mentioned in the context of Jesus choosing all twelve disciples to be His closest followers and to be sent out to preach and perform miracles (Mark 3:14-19).

Each disciple's call highlights Jesus' diverse selection, emphasizing that He chose ordinary people from various backgrounds to follow Him and carry forward His mission. Just two words—"follow me"—were sufficient for these men to leave everything and follow Jesus, demonstrating the authoritative and charismatic presence of Jesus from the onset of His ministry.

After selecting them, Jesus empowered the twelve with the authority to preach about the kingdom of God and to heal the sick. This empowerment extended beyond simple task delegation; it was an invitation to share in His mission. He educated them not just through verbal teachings but through direct life experiences, showing what it means to love unconditionally, serve with humility, and stand strong in faith.

The disciples were firsthand witnesses to Jesus' miracles, His compassion towards the needy, His bold confrontations with religious authorities, and His moments of deep prayer and solitude. They were integral to major events such as the Sermon on the Mount, the miraculous feeding of thousands, and ultimately the profound occurrences of the crucifixion and resurrection.

Selecting these twelve also mirrored the scriptural motif of the twelve tribes of Israel, symbolizing a fresh start in God's plan for salvation. Jesus was not just forming a group of followers; He was establishing a new spiritual family that would break past traditional ethnic and social boundaries, united under faith in Him. This group would lay the foundational stones of the Church, tasked with spreading the gospel of Jesus Christ to every corner of the globe, echoing His teachings and His love across nations and generations.

The Sermon on the Mount

One of the most pivotal and enlightening segments of Jesus' ministry is encapsulated in the Sermon on the Mount. Detailed in Matthew chapters 5 through 7, this sermon captures Jesus as He imparts divine wisdom on a mountainside, surrounded by His disciples and a multitude of followers. His words, rich with spiritual depth, continue to resonate and challenge individuals across the ages.

The sermon initiates with the Beatitudes—profound blessings for those embodying specific virtues or facing particular hardships: "Blessed are the poor in spirit, for theirs is the kingdom of heaven. Blessed are those who mourn, for they will be comforted" (Matthew 5:3-4). These declarations flip conventional values on their head, illustrating that true fulfillment and blessing stem not from earthly riches or power but from a life attuned to God's principles.

Jesus further exhorts His followers to be salt and light in the world, urging them to positively influence the world while preserving their distinctiveness as God's people. He clarifies that His mission is not to overthrow the Law or the Prophets but to complete them (Matthew 5:17), bridging His teachings with the Old Testament and encouraging a deeper, more comprehensive application of God's commandments.

Central to the sermon is the call for a righteousness that exceeds that of the Pharisees and teachers of the law. Jesus challenges His audience to pursue a righteousness that transcends mere external adherence to rules, advocating for a heart transformation that permeates every aspect of life. He addresses everyday behaviors and attitudes, ranging from handling anger and lust to the principles of love, generosity, prayer, and forgiveness. For instance, His command to "love your enemies and pray for those who persecute you" (Matthew 5:44) stretches traditional notions of love and righteousness.

Included in His sermon is the Lord's Prayer, a succinct yet profound blueprint for prayer that emphasizes God's sovereignty, our dependence on Him for our daily needs, the forgiveness of sins, and deliverance from evil. This prayer underscores a relational approach to God that balances reverence with intimate dependency.

Jesus also speaks against the perils of materialism, encouraging His followers to accumulate treasures in heaven rather than on earth, where decay and theft can prevail (Matthew 6:19-20). He stresses the importance of prioritizing God's kingdom and trusting Him to provide for our necessities.

The sermon culminates with a compelling call to action. Jesus likens those who hear His words and act on them to a wise builder whose house, founded on rock, withstands storms. Conversely, those who hear but do not act are compared to a foolish builder whose house collapses under adversity (Matthew 7:24-27).

This sermon not only challenges our perspectives, actions, and priorities but also invites us to align them with God's will. Through these teachings, Jesus beckons us to experience the fullness of life under God's reign, offering timeless guidance that transcends cultural and temporal boundaries. It is a call to live by the spirit of the law, fostering a transformative relationship with God that reshapes our very being.

The Teachings

Beyond the seminal Sermon on the Mount, Jesus' teachings span a broad array of topics and parables, each unveiling deep truths about the kingdom of God, the essence of love, and the route to true fulfillment. These teachings, delivered with unmatched authority and compassion, continue to influence and guide millions globally.

A central theme in Jesus' instruction is the command to love profoundly and expansively. Jesus distills the essence of the Law and the Prophets into two commandments in Mark 12:30-31: love God with all your heart, soul, mind, and strength, and love your neighbor as yourself. This revolutionary notion of love even extends to enemies and persecutors, urging His followers to demonstrate a level of love and forgiveness that surpasses ordinary human inclinations toward retaliation or bitterness (Matthew 5:44).

Jesus often employed parables to communicate spiritual truths, making complex ideas accessible to everyone. For example, the Parable of the Prodigal Son (Luke 15:11-32) highlights God's limitless mercy and His joy at the return of a repentant sinner, reassuring us of God's readiness to forgive and celebrate our return, no matter our missteps.

Another pivotal teaching of Jesus concerns judgment. Through the Parable of the Good Samaritan (Luke 10:25-37), Jesus overturns societal norms and prejudices, showing that true acts of neighborly kindness transcend national or social boundaries. He also warns against hypocritical judgment, promoting a spirit of self-reflection and humility before God (Matthew 7:1-5).

Furthermore, Jesus addresses faith and prayer extensively. He points out the transformative power of even a small amount of faith—comparable to a mustard seed—in moving mountains (Matthew 17:20), encouraging His followers to rely on God's provision and oversight. Through the Lord's Prayer (Matthew 6:9-13), He models a comprehensive approach to prayer that includes praise, confession, gratitude, and petition, emphasizing the importance of prioritizing God's kingdom and will.

Jesus also vividly describes the kingdom of God using various parables to portray its paradoxical and surprising nature. For example, the Parables of the Hidden Treasure and the Pearl of Great Price (Matthew 13:44-46) depict the kingdom's immense value, worthy of sacrificing everything else to obtain.

In discussing the perils of wealth and the importance of generosity, Jesus' interaction with the Rich Young Man (Matthew 19:16-24) highlights the spiritual dangers of wealth, underscoring that eternal life and heavenly treasures far outweigh earthly riches.

Crucially, Jesus exemplified the principles he taught through His daily interactions. His engagements with the marginalized, His empathy towards the sick and sinners, and His ultimate sacrifice on the cross epitomize His teachings. Jesus' teachings not only instruct but also challenge us to scrutinize our hearts, transform our interactions, and make a positive impact on the world. They provide a blueprint for living a life pleasing to God, marked by love, humility, and a pursuit of righteousness.

Redefining the Law

A pivotal moment in Jesus Christ's ministry is when He distilled the essence of the law and the prophets into two commandments. This significant teaching moment underscores His role as the fulfiller of the law, simplifying complex legalistic traditions into principles rooted deeply in love and compassion.

The context of this teaching is captured vividly in the Gospels, where Jesus, engaging with the Pharisees, succinctly summarizes the entirety of the Old Testament commandments into two foundational principles. As recorded in Matthew 22:37-40, Jesus says, "'Love the Lord your God with all your heart and with all your soul and with all your mind.' This is the first and greatest commandment. And the second is like it: 'Love your neighbor as yourself.' All the Law and the Prophets hang on these two commandments." This profound statement not only highlights the centrality of love in Christian ethics but also redefines the approach to religious observance from a legalistic adherence to a spirit-led embodiment of love.

The first commandment Jesus refers to is rooted in Deuteronomy 6:5, emphasizing total and complete love for God. This is not just a call to emotional affection but a comprehensive commitment involving every aspect of one's being: heart, soul, and mind. It challenges believers to prioritize their relationship with God above all else, aligning every aspect of their lives with His will.

I must address the importance of the first commandment, as some people embrace the command to love their neighbor but struggle with the directive to love God, finding issue with the reference to 'God' as the lawgiver. It is essential to recognize that without a lawgiver, there can be no law. Therefore, objections to loving God miss the foundational point of the commandments. To claim one can love their neighbor without loving God is analogous to a child saying they appreciate their parent's friends but not the parent themselves. Such a stance undermines the coherence and integrity of the commandments. The first commandment is not just about a duty; it is about recognizing and honoring the source of all moral authority. Loving God is not an arbitrary decree; it is foundational to genuine and holistic moral behavior, integrating our deepest commitments and affections with the divine will that shapes them.

The second commandment, drawn from Leviticus 19:18, extends the concept of love to interpersonal relationships. It calls for a selfless and sacrificial love towards others, reflecting the love one has for oneself. This commandment is revolutionary because it encapsulates a universal principle of empathy and kindness, cutting across cultural, social, and religious barriers to promote a community built on mutual respect and care.

The understanding of the second commandment, as drawn from Leviticus 19:18, requires a deeper exploration to correct common misconceptions, particularly among Christians, which I believe has contributed to the decline of Christianity in its historical strongholds. This commandment urges us to love others selflessly and sacrificially, reflecting the love we hold for ourselves. It is revolutionary, promoting empathy and kindness across all human divides. However, it is crucial to clarify that this command to love does not equate to compromising our core beliefs. Jesus embodied this love perfectly; He dined with sinners and forgave those who crucified Him, yet He never wavered from His divine mission. His crucifixion, death, and resurrection are non-negotiable truths that form the foundation of Christianity.

THE LIFE OF CHRIST JESUS

Today, some interfaith dialogues and efforts to find 'common ground' have led to concessions that dilute these essential truths, such as acknowledging Jesus merely as a prophet rather than recognizing His divinity. This trend is profoundly troubling—it represents a fundamental departure from the bedrock of Christian faith. By accepting and even promoting views that deny Jesus' crucifixion, divinity, and resurrection, these individuals essentially betray the very essence of Christianity. It is akin to saying, 'It's acceptable for you to reject the central tenets of my faith, and I will not only accept your view but advocate it within my community.'

This compromise under the guise of tolerance and unity undermines the truth of the Gospel and raises a crucial question: can one truly identify as Christian while denying the divinity and resurrection of Christ, the core of our faith? Such concessions are not acts of love or unity but of profound misguidance, leading believers astray from the true teachings of Jesus as revealed in the Scriptures.

This is a profound error, mistaking compromise for love. True Christian love involves standing firm in our faith while extending grace and understanding, not relinquishing our foundational beliefs. As we will discuss in a later chapter, recognizing Jesus as God is not just an aspect of faith; it is the cornerstone of all Christian doctrine.

Jesus' redefinition of the law through these two commandments was radical. It confronted the prevailing religious norms that often burdened people with intricate rules and rituals, which sometimes led to legalism that overshadowed the law's original intent. By emphasizing love as the fulfillment of the law, Jesus pointed to the heart's transformation as more crucial than mere external compliance.

Teaching to Pray

Jesus also taught how to pray. The disciples asked Jesus to teach them to pray, recognizing their need to deepen their spiritual communication. Jesus' response, including the Lord's Prayer, provides not only a template for prayer but profound insights into the nature of our relationship with God.

Jesus begins by teaching His disciples the Lord's Prayer, as recorded in Matthew 6:9-13. This prayer encapsulates the essence of what prayer should encompass: reverence for God, acknowledgment of His kingdom, submission to His will, reliance on Him for daily needs, and a plea for forgiveness and deliverance from evil. Each component of this prayer guides believers in seeking a balanced spiritual life, emphasizing dependence on God's providence and mercy.

In this prayer, Jesus starts with "Our Father in heaven, hallowed be your name," a phrase that elevates the sanctity and sovereignty of God. This acknowledgment of God's holiness sets the tone for the respect and reverence due in our prayers. He then addresses the coming of God's kingdom and the fulfillment of His will on earth as in heaven, aligning our desires with God's eternal purposes rather than our transient wishes.

Following this, Jesus covers daily sustenance and spiritual needs—"Give us today our daily bread. And forgive us our debts, as we also have forgiven our debtors." Here, Jesus touches on the physical provision and spiritual grace essential for daily living. This part of the prayer reflects our dependence on God for both material and moral support, reminding us of our need for His continual presence in our lives.

THE LIFE OF CHRIST JESUS

Jesus concludes the prayer with a request for spiritual guidance and protection: "And lead us not into temptation, but deliver us from the evil one." This petition recognizes the reality of spiritual adversity and the need for divine assistance to overcome trials and temptations.

Beyond the Lord's Prayer, Jesus also emphasizes the manner and attitude one should adopt while praying. In Matthew 6:5-6, He advises against praying to be seen by others, critiquing those who use prayer as a means to gain public admiration. Instead, He instructs His followers to pray in private, entering into a secluded space and closing the door. This guidance encourages a personal, intimate dialogue with God, free from pretense and distraction.

Jesus further warns against mindless blabbering and empty phrases, cautioning against the belief that verbosity ensures being heard. Instead, He reassures His followers that God knows their needs before they even ask (Matthew 6:7-8). This instruction redirects the focus from the quantity of words to the quality of the heart's posture during prayer.

The teachings of Jesus on prayer are not merely rituals or formulas but are profound invitations to engage sincerely with God. They highlight the importance of humility, sincerity, and a focus on God's kingdom in our prayers. These principles are not just theological concepts but are meant to be lived out, transforming our prayer life into a meaningful and dynamic interaction with God. They challenge believers to reflect on their motives and attitudes in prayer, ensuring that this spiritual discipline remains a genuine expression of faith and dependence on God.

The Miracles

Jesus performed numerous miracles throughout His ministry, demonstrating His divine power and compassion. The Gospels record thirty-seven distinct miracles, each highlighting a different aspect of His ability to heal, provide, protect, and demonstrate authority over the natural and spiritual realms, and even death, showcasing His deep care for humanity and His ultimate control over creation. These miraculous acts were not merely displays of power; they were significant signs that affirmed Jesus' identity as the Son of God and heralded the arrival of God's kingdom.

The earliest recorded miracle Jesus performed was at a wedding in Cana, where He transformed water into wine (John 2:1-11). This miracle at a simple family celebration highlighted Jesus' concern for human joy and needs, indicating that no concern is too small for His attention. It also served as a sign of His glory, deepening the faith of His disciples.

Jesus' healing miracles are particularly renowned. He addressed a wide range of ailments, restoring health and wholeness with acts that not only displayed divine power but also had societal implications. For instance, by touching and healing a man with leprosy—a condition that rendered individuals social outcasts—Jesus demonstrated a profound breaking of social barriers (Matthew 8:2-3). He also gave sight to the blind and mobility to the paralyzed, such as when He healed a man born blind (John 9:1-12) and another paralyzed for 38 years (John 5:5-9), thus restoring their dignity and societal roles.

His command over nature is vividly illustrated when He calmed a storm on the Sea of Galilee (Mark 4:39). As His disciples panicked,

THE LIFE OF CHRIST JESUS

Jesus simply spoke, and the wind and waves ceased, showcasing His sovereignty over the physical world. Similarly, the feeding of over 5,000 people with just five loaves and two fish (Matthew 14:13-21) emphasized His ability to provide bountifully, echoing the providence of God for His people.

Among His most awe-inspiring miracles was the raising of Lazarus from the dead (John 11:43-44). This act was not just a comfort to the bereaved but also a potent symbol of hope and a preview of the resurrection power that Jesus Himself would demonstrate, offering life beyond the grave.

The broader significance of Jesus' miracles transcends their immediate impact. Each miracle was a signpost pointing to the dawning of God's kingdom—a realm where pain, suffering, and death will be eradicated, and where divine rule brings perpetual healing, provision, and peace. These miracles encouraged faith not just in the miraculous acts themselves but in Jesus as the Messiah and the Son of God, inviting all to believe in Him and the eternal life He offers.

Of all the miracles Jesus performed, His own resurrection stands unparalleled as the greatest miracle, definitively proving His divine nature. By triumphing over death itself, Jesus not only fulfilled numerous prophecies but also demonstrated ultimate authority and power, distinguishing Him categorically from any other figure in human history. This singular event—His victory over the grave—is the cornerstone of Christian faith, affirming His identity as God incarnate. The resurrection is the ultimate testament to Jesus' claim to divinity, offering hope and redemption to humanity, confirming that He is truly the Son of God who conquered death, promising eternal life to all who believe in Him.

The Parables

The parables of Jesus are central to His teachings, vividly illustrating spiritual truths through simple, engaging stories. The Gospels record forty parables that cover themes such as the kingdom of God, forgiveness, grace, compassion, and the impending judgment. These narratives use everyday life scenarios to make complex spiritual lessons accessible to everyone, regardless of social standing or education. Often featuring an unexpected twist, each parable challenges its listeners to reflect and take action.

One iconic parable is that of the Prodigal Son (Luke 15:11-32). This story of a young man who squanders his inheritance and returns home in disgrace only to be warmly embraced by his father beautifully illustrates God's boundless grace and forgiveness. It highlights that no one is beyond redemption and celebrates the joy in heaven over each repentant sinner.

Another profound narrative is the Good Samaritan (Luke 10:30-37), which tells of a man beaten and left for dead, passed by religious leaders but helped by a Samaritan, who was despised by societal elites. This parable redefines neighborly love, showing that true compassion knows no boundaries of race or social status. It calls for mercy and kindness towards all, especially those marginalized or overlooked by society.

The Parable of the Sower (Matthew 13:3-23) compares the reception of God's word to seeds falling on different types of soil, representing the condition of our hearts. It encourages believers to prepare their hearts to receive God's word, allowing it to grow and produce a fruitful harvest.

THE LIFE OF CHRIST JESUS

In the Parable of the Talents (Matthew 25:14-30), Jesus describes a man who entrusts his property to his servants. This story stresses the importance of using God-given gifts wisely, illustrating that faithful stewardship of small responsibilities can lead to greater opportunities.

Jesus' parables are timeless, touching on universal aspects of the human experience and offering guidance for living a life aligned with God's values. Each story invites listeners into a deeper understanding of God's character and kingdom, urging a transformation that aligns more closely with divine principles.

Through these stories, Jesus demonstrated masterful storytelling skills, captivating His listeners and engaging their hearts and minds. These narratives continue to inspire, challenge, and comfort people around the world, encouraging them to discover and live out the truths of the gospel. The parables of Jesus teach us that divine truths are often hidden in plain sight, awaiting discovery by those who are ready to listen and change.

The Transfiguration

The Transfiguration stands as one of the most striking events in Jesus' public ministry, vividly depicted in the Gospels of Matthew, Mark, and Luke. This event powerfully underscores Jesus' divine nature and His role in God's redemptive plan, providing His closest disciples with a glimpse of His glory.

Jesus took Peter, James, and John up a high mountain, a place away from the daily thrum of life. There, something extraordinary happened: Jesus' appearance was transformed. His face shone like the sun, and His clothes became dazzling white (Matthew 17:2). This was not merely a visual change but a profound revelation of the divine glory that Jesus possessed, temporarily revealing His true heavenly nature amidst His earthly mission.

The scene is enriched with the appearance of Moses and Elijah, representing the Law and the Prophets. Their presence with Jesus not only signifies that He is the fulfillment of both the Law and the prophetic messages but also underscores His central role in God's salvation history. They discuss His "departure," which refers to His upcoming suffering, death, and resurrection in Jerusalem (Luke 9:31), pivotal events for humanity's redemption.

During this miraculous event, God's voice is heard from a cloud, affirming Jesus' identity: "This is my Son, whom I love; with him I am well pleased. Listen to him!" (Matthew 17:5). This echoes the affirmation at Jesus' baptism and serves as a divine command to heed Jesus' teachings, emphasizing His authority and the critical nature of His mission.

The disciples' reaction is one of sheer terror and awe. Peter, ever impulsive, suggests building three shelters for Jesus, Moses, and Elijah—an attempt to prolong the heavenly encounter. However, the divine voice from the cloud redirects their attention solely to Jesus, underscoring His preeminence over the Law and the Prophets.

When the disciples hear this voice, they fall face down to the ground, overwhelmed by fear. Jesus' comforting touch and command not to be afraid reassures them. This interaction highlights Jesus' role as the mediator between God and man, His compassion, and His readiness to guide and support His followers.

The Transfiguration not only fortifies the disciples' faith, giving them a vision of Jesus' glory that would sustain them through the upcoming trials of His crucifixion and death but also solidifies Jesus' identity as the Messiah. It offers a compelling glimpse into the glory that Jesus, though fully human during His ministry, held as the divine Son of God. This moment is a testament to His ultimate victory over death and His forthcoming resurrection, providing both a reason for hope and a foundation for faith.

The Triumphal Entry

The Triumphal Entry of Jesus into Jerusalem is a pivotal event in His earthly ministry, marking the beginning of the final week leading up to His crucifixion and resurrection. This event, depicted in all four Gospels, symbolizes Jesus' declaration of His messianic identity, not through force or grandeur, but through humility.

Jesus approached Jerusalem, the heart of Jewish religious life, in a manner that fulfilled the prophecy of Zechariah: "See, your king comes to you, gentle and riding on a donkey, on a colt, the foal of a donkey" (Zechariah 9:9). By choosing to ride on a donkey, Jesus symbolized peace rather than conquest, subverting common expectations of a Messiah who would overthrow Roman oppression with military might.

As He rode into the city, the crowds responded with jubilant celebration. They spread their cloaks and palm branches on the road, creating a royal pathway. The air rang with shouts of "Hosanna to the Son of David!" and "Blessed is he who comes in the name of the Lord! Hosanna in the highest heaven!" (Matthew 21:9). The term "Hosanna" originally meant 'save now,' but on this occasion, it was a joyous acclamation of Jesus' arrival, recognizing Him as the promised deliverer.

However, not everyone received Jesus with praise. The city was stirred, and some were perplexed about His identity, asking, "Who is this?" The religious leaders, observing the adoration Jesus received, felt threatened and indignant. They were disturbed not only by the crowd's acceptance of Jesus as the messianic king but also by the potential ramifications of His popularity under the watchful eyes of the Roman authorities.

THE LIFE OF CHRIST JESUS

Jesus' entry into Jerusalem was more than a fulfillment of prophecy; it was a profound declaration of His kingship's nature. He entered as a king of peace and humility, directly challenging the prevailing expectations of a political liberator. This approach highlighted the spiritual essence of His kingdom, which contrasted sharply with the earthly kingdoms that relied on power and oppression.

This moment also intensified the unfolding drama that would lead to Jesus' passion. In the days that followed, He would cleanse the temple, confront the religious authorities, and speak openly about the destruction of Jerusalem and the final judgment. These actions would further cement the opposition against Him, setting the stage for the dramatic events of His crucifixion.

THE PASSION WEEK

This section covers the following topics:

- *Introduction*
- *Cleansing of the Temple*
- *Confrontations with Religious Leaders*
- *Teaching in the Temple*
- *The Olivet Discourse*
- *A Friend Agrees to Betray*
- *The Last Supper*
- *In the Garden of Gethsemane*
- *The Betrayal and Arrest*
- *The Condemnation*
- *The Denial of Peter*
- *Trial before Pilate*
- *Sent to Herod*
- *Sentenced to Death*
- *The Torture*
- *The Crucifixion*

Introduction

The Passion Week marks the culmination of Jesus Christ's earthly ministry, a period dense with emotional and spiritual milestones that define Christian faith. During this sacred week, from His triumphant entry into Jerusalem to His crucifixion and resurrection, every event meticulously unfolds to reveal the depth of God's plan for human redemption.

The week starts with a poignant moment of purification and confrontation; Jesus cleanses the Temple, reclaiming it as a house of prayer and challenging the entrenched hypocrisy of the religious leaders. This act of cleansing is both literal and symbolic, setting the stage for His final teachings about truth and justice, captured in the profound conversations of the Olivet Discourse.

The shadow of betrayal looms large as Judas Iscariot agrees to betray Jesus for thirty pieces of silver, a poignant fulfillment of the prophecies about the Messiah's suffering. This betrayal introduces a cascade of events that lead directly to the cross, highlighting the painful reality of human betrayal and sin.

One of the most intimate moments of the week is the Last Supper, where Jesus shares bread and wine with His disciples, establishing the sacrament of Communion. He presents these elements as His body and blood, symbols of His impending sacrifice. This supper serves as a covenant, a reminder to His followers to continually remember the sacrifice He was about to make for the sins of the world.

In the Garden of Gethsemane, Jesus' humanity and divinity intersect profoundly. His prayer, "Not my will, but yours be done," reflects His submission to the divine will, despite the overwhelming anguish that caused Him to sweat blood. This moment of intense agony underscores the enormity of what Jesus was prepared to endure, affirming His obedience and love for humanity.

The narrative continues through the dark hours of Jesus' arrest, trials before Pilate and Herod, and Peter's heartbreaking denial. Each event fulfills ancient messianic prophecies and contrasts human frailty with divine sovereignty. Peter's denial, in particular, highlights the struggle between fear and faith, serving as a powerful lesson in human fallibility and divine forgiveness.

The journey to Calvary is the apex of Jesus' physical and spiritual suffering. Carrying the cross, He embodies the weight of the world's sins. His crucifixion is marked by both cruelty and mercy, His final words offering forgiveness to those who crucified Him, "Father, forgive them, for they do not know what they are doing." The tearing of the temple veil at His death symbolizes the removal of the barrier between God and humanity, signifying that all people can now directly access the divine presence.

Jesus' final moments and His recognition by a Roman centurion as the "Son of God" encapsulate the transformative impact of His mission, transcending religious boundaries and offering salvation to all of humanity.

The Passion Week is more than a historical account; it is a narrative of ultimate sacrifice and profound love. Each event invites believers to reflect on the magnitude of Jesus' sacrifice and the transformative power of His love, culminating in His victory over sin and death. This week is the core of the Gospel, offering each of us deep insights into the character of Christ and the expansive nature of God's redeeming love.

Cleansing of the Temple

In the heart of Jerusalem, within the sacred walls of the Temple, Jesus Christ executed a powerful and symbolic act: the Cleansing of the Temple. This decisive moment is detailed across the Gospels—Matthew 21:12-13, Mark 11:15-17, and Luke 19:45-46—showcasing Jesus' dedication to the sanctity of worship and His rejection of the commercialization of religious practices.

Upon entering the Temple, Jesus encountered a scene that contradicted the very essence of its purpose. The Temple, designated as a place for prayer and communion with God, was cluttered with merchants and money changers. These individuals had turned a sacred space into a bustling market, selling animals for sacrifices and exchanging money, which was necessary for paying the Temple tax in the appropriate currency. Witnessing this, Jesus responded with righteous anger, overturning the tables and clearing the Temple of these commercial activities. His forceful actions made a clear statement: the house of God was not to be a place of profit.

Through this act, Jesus invoked the words of Isaiah, emphasizing that the Temple should be a "house of prayer" but had been turned into a "den of robbers" (Matthew 21:13). This rebuke was not merely a critique of the merchants but a profound denunciation of the religious leaders who allowed worship to be overshadowed by monetary gain.

The Cleansing of the Temple is significant not only for its immediate impact but also for its deeper theological implications. It challenged prevailing religious norms and pointed to the corruption that had seeped into religious practices. Jesus called for worship that was genuine and free from the taint of hypocrisy and greed. This event foreshadowed the new covenant, where true worship would not be confined to the physical temple but would transcend to a spiritual plane, where Jesus himself would be the cornerstone.

Furthermore, this episode underscored Jesus' role as a reformer and his authority to redefine the essence of true worship. It highlighted his commitment to purifying religious practice, ensuring that it reflected the sincerity and purity essential to true devotion.

For believers today, the Cleansing of the Temple serves as a potent reminder of the importance of preserving the sanctity of worship spaces. It calls for introspection and vigilance to ensure that our religious practices remain sincere and focused on God, free from the distractions and distortions of external influences. This narrative continues to resonate, urging us to reflect on our own practices and to seek a relationship with God that is rooted in authenticity and heartfelt devotion.

Confrontations with Religious Leaders

During the final days before His crucifixion, Jesus Christ engaged in pivotal confrontations with the religious leaders of Jerusalem, as detailed across the Gospels. These encounters were not merely debates; they were profound illustrations of Jesus' dedication to unveiling truth and promoting justice against entrenched religious hypocrisy.

One notable confrontation occurred over the issue of taxation, where Pharisees and Herodians attempted to trap Jesus with a question about paying taxes to Caesar. Using a coin as a prop, Jesus asked whose image was on it. When they responded "Caesar's," He delivered a timeless principle: "So give back to Caesar what is Caesar's, and to God what is God's" (Matthew 22:21). This response brilliantly highlighted the separation of civic and spiritual responsibilities, showcasing Jesus' wisdom and refusal to be entrapped by their cunning.

Another significant encounter was with the Sadducees, who denied the resurrection. They posed a hypothetical question about marriage in the afterlife to challenge Jesus. He corrected their misunderstanding, emphasizing that "He is not the God of the dead, but of the living" (Matthew 22:32 NIV), thus affirming the reality of resurrection and the continuity of life beyond death.

The Pharisees also tested Jesus by asking which commandment was the greatest. Jesus' response encapsulated the heart of the Mosaic Law: to love God wholly and to love one's neighbor as oneself (Matthew 22:37-39). This succinct summary underscored that genuine faith is rooted in love, surpassing ritualistic observances.

These confrontations with the religious leaders served multiple purposes. They exposed the leaders' superficial adherence to the law, which often masked a deeper spiritual emptiness. Jesus used these moments not only to defend against accusations but also to teach profound truths about faith, righteousness, and the kingdom of God. His responses revealed His deep respect for the law, paired with a clarion call for a return to its true, loving purposes.

By consistently pointing back to the heart of God's commandments, Jesus positioned Himself as a reformer. His unflinching stance against the distortions of the religious elite not only escalated their animosity towards Him but also solidified His role as the Messiah who came not to abolish the law but to fulfill it.

These rigorous exchanges underscored Jesus' commitment to truth and justice, challenging wrong interpretations and practices. They emphasize His role as a transformative leader, whose teachings continue to challenge and guide believers towards living out the essence of God's laws in their lives.

Teaching in the Temple

After His triumphant entry into Jerusalem, Jesus transformed the temple from a mere place of worship into a dynamic forum for education and spiritual challenge. During these crucial days of Holy Week, Jesus not only acted as a teacher but also as a prophetic voice, articulating profound truths that cut to the heart of religious law and pointed towards the imminent establishment of the Kingdom of God.

Jesus' teachings in the temple included powerful parables such as the Parable of the Tenants (Matthew 21:33-46), where he described tenants who betray and murder the son of their landowner, symbolizing the religious leaders' looming betrayal of Christ Himself. This parable was a direct confrontation, exposing the leaders' corruption and forecasting the grave consequences of their actions. Through this story, Jesus positioned Himself as the cornerstone of God's salvific plan, essential and unavoidable.

During these temple sessions, Jesus emphasized the core commandments: loving God wholeheartedly and loving one's neighbor as oneself (Matthew 22:34-40). This teaching distilled the essence of the law into actions driven by love, challenging His listeners to adopt a more profound moral and spiritual ethos that transcended mere ritual compliance.

One of the most intense moments was Jesus' open denouncement of the religious leaders' hypocrisy (Matthew 23). He criticized their superficial piety which lacked substance in justice, mercy, and faithfulness, urging a return to the true intentions of God's commands. This critique was not merely to admonish but to spur true repentance and spiritual renewal.

Jesus also spoke prophetically about the future, particularly predicting the temple's destruction, linking it to wider themes of divine judgment and ultimate redemption (Matthew 24). His prophecies served as both a warning and a beacon of hope, calling for vigilance and steadfast faith in the face of trials.

These teachings in the temple illustrate how Jesus used this central religious setting to clarify His mission and lay down the tenets of the Kingdom He proclaimed. He redefined the understanding of divine requirements, emphasizing an internal transformation that leads to broader societal and global change.

By positioning Himself as a prophetic figure in the temple, Jesus challenged the status quo and called everyone to a deeper, more meaningful engagement with God. His teachings continue to resonate, urging ongoing reflection and a commitment to embodying the values of God's Kingdom in every aspect of life.

The Olivet Discourse

After His triumphal entry into Jerusalem and before the solemnity of Holy Thursday, Jesus delivered a pivotal teaching known as the Olivet Discourse. This profound sermon, detailed in the synoptic Gospels, occurred on the Mount of Olives with a panoramic view of the Temple. Here, Jesus foretold the destruction of Jerusalem and the temple, and elaborated on the signs that would herald the end times and His eventual return, weaving prophecy with vital admonitions.

The discourse opened with Jesus' dramatic prophecy that not a single stone of the Temple would remain intact; all would be toppled (Matthew 24:2). This stark prediction prefaced a broader discussion about future trials, describing wars, famines, earthquakes, and persecutions as the beginning of sorrows—pains leading to a new era (Matthew 24:6-8).

Within these prophecies, Jesus stressed vigilance and readiness. He cautioned His disciples to guard against deceit by false prophets and messiahs, capable of impressive wonders meant to lead many astray (Matthew 24:24). His emphasis was not on instilling fear but on preparing His followers for the forthcoming challenges, encouraging them to persist in faith and remain watchful for His return.

A compelling feature of the Olivet Discourse is Jesus' use of parables to underscore His teachings. He employed the Parable of the Fig Tree (Matthew 24:32-35) to illustrate that just as one can predict summer's arrival by observing the fig tree, so too can one interpret the signs of significant forthcoming events. He further conveyed the importance of preparedness through the Parable of the Wise and Foolish Virgins

(Matthew 25:1-13) and advocated for diligent stewardship in the Parable of the Talents (Matthew 25:14-30).

The discourse culminates with the Parable of the Sheep and the Goats (Matthew 25:31-46), a vivid depiction of the final judgment that separates humanity based on their actions of compassion and mercy. This narrative underscores the moral imperatives of His kingdom.

The Olivet Discourse serves not only as a prophetic outline but as a directive for ethical living and spiritual vigilance. It calls followers to transcend immediate political and social upheavals by focusing on the eternal kingdom of God, promoting a life of alertness, morality, and unwavering faithfulness to His teachings.

This teaching encapsulates dual themes of caution and hope—alerting followers to the trials and deceptive doctrines ahead, while promising the ultimate realization of God's kingdom. Through this seminal discourse, Jesus assures us that despite temporal turmoil, His return will restore order, ensuring justice and peace prevail.

A Friend Agrees to Betray

In the poignant narrative of Jesus' final days, one of the most dramatic and disheartening events is the betrayal by His disciple, Judas Iscariot. This episode underscores profound themes of human frailty, the struggle between temptation and morality, and the intricate fulfillment of ancient prophecies.

Judas Iscariot, one of the Twelve Apostles, made a conscious decision to betray Jesus to the religious leaders who were looking for a clandestine way to arrest and execute Him. The religious leaders sought to avoid public upheaval, as Jesus was widely followed and admired by many. Judas approached them, offering to hand over Jesus in exchange for money, setting the stage for one of the most infamous acts of treachery in history.

The Gospel of Matthew chillingly details this transaction, noting Judas' question, "What are you willing to give me if I deliver him over to you?" (Matthew 26:15). The priests agreed to pay him thirty pieces of silver, an amount prophesied in Zechariah 11:12-13 as the deplorable price set on Jesus' life. This sum starkly symbolizes the tragic undervaluation of the Savior's worth.

Judas then looked for an opportunity to betray Jesus discreetly, planning to identify Him with a kiss—an act that would later unfold in the Garden of Gethsemane. This betrayal was not an impulsive decision but a premeditated act, illustrating the depth of human duplicity and calculation.

This act of betrayal serves not only as a testament to the frailty of the human heart but also highlights the importance of steadfastness in faith and the dangers of succumbing to greed and despair. It also poignantly underscores the depth of Jesus' sacrifice—showing his profound love and forgiveness, even in the face of betrayal. Despite knowing Judas' plan, Jesus still shared the Last Supper with him, offering him the same grace extended to all His disciples.

The Last Supper

The Last Supper marks not only the final meal Jesus shared with His disciples before His crucifixion but also a pivotal moment of profound spiritual legacy. Recorded in the Gospels, this event forms the foundation of the Eucharist or Communion, a central act of Christian worship. During this meal, Jesus imparted significant teachings about service, sacrifice, and the new covenant between God and humanity.

Taking place during the Passover festival, a time commemorating the Israelites' liberation from Egyptian slavery, Jesus gathered with His twelve disciples in an upper room in Jerusalem. This setting of liberation and covenant profoundly underscored Jesus' revelation of His mission. As they dined, Jesus took bread, gave thanks, broke it, and distributed it, saying, "This is my body given for you; do this in remembrance of me" (Luke 22:19). Similarly, after the meal, He took the cup and declared, "This cup is the new covenant in my blood, which is poured out for you" (Luke 22:20). These actions not only anticipated His imminent death on the cross but also instituted a new covenant, fulfilling Old Testament prophecies and offering a promise of salvation and eternal life made possible through His sacrifice.

This event, coupled with Jesus' command to 'do this in remembrance of me,' established the basis for the Eucharist or Communion. This sacrament, observed by Christians worldwide, not only commemorates Jesus' sacrifice but also actively unites believers in a common faith, serving as a continuous reminder of His enduring presence and sacrifice.

At the Last Supper, Jesus set a new standard for service. He washed the feet of His disciples, an act of humility and service that inverted conventional social hierarchies. This act, recorded in John's Gospel, exemplified the selfless love and service Jesus expected from His followers. "Now that I, your Lord and Teacher, have washed your feet, you also should wash one another's feet. I have set you an example that you should do as I have done for you" (John 13:14-15). This teaching emphasized that true greatness in His kingdom is found in serving others.

Moreover, the Last Supper was a poignant moment of revelation and sorrow. Jesus disclosed that one of the disciples would betray Him, leading to His arrest and crucifixion. He also solemnly forewarned them, "This very night you will all fall away on account of me, for it is written: 'I will strike the shepherd, and the sheep of the flock will be scattered.' But after I have risen, I will go ahead of you into Galilee."

Peter, troubled by this prediction, protested, "Even if all fall away on account of you, I never will." To this, Jesus replied, "I tell you the truth," Jesus answered, "this very night, before the rooster crows, you will disown me three times." Yet Peter insisted, "Even if I have to die with you, I will never disown you." And all the other disciples echoed his sentiment (Matthew 26: 31-35).

The Last Supper encapsulates the essence of Jesus' ministry and the heart of the Christian gospel. It signifies the transition from the old covenant, centered on law and sacrifice, to the new covenant, founded on grace and the ultimate sacrifice of Jesus.

In the Garden of Gethsemane

In the Garden of Gethsemane, after the Last Supper, Jesus and His disciples went to a place where He frequently went for prayer and reflection. Luke vividly captures the intensity of Jesus' agony there, describing how He withdrew about a stone's throw beyond them, knelt down and prayed, 'Father, if you are willing, take this cup from me; yet not my will, but yours be done.' An angel from heaven appeared to Him and strengthened Him. In deep anguish, He prayed more earnestly, and His sweat was like drops of blood falling to the ground (Luke 22:41-44).

Matthew's Gospel provides further details, showing that, aware of the impending events, Jesus took Peter, James, and John deeper into the garden. He expressed His profound distress to them, saying, 'My soul is overwhelmed with sorrow to the point of death. Stay here and keep watch with me' (Matthew 26:38). This confession underscores the depth of Jesus' humanity and the reality of His struggle.

Alone in prayer, Jesus repeatedly besought His Father, saying, 'My Father, if it is possible, may this cup be taken from me. Yet not as I will, but as you will' (Matthew 26:39). He made this plea three times, highlighting His desire to avoid suffering yet reaffirming His resolve to adhere to God's plan, whatever the cost. This represented a moment of total submission to God's will, reflecting Jesus' deep obedience and faith.

Meanwhile, the disciples struggled to stay awake, falling asleep despite Jesus' repeated requests for them to remain vigilant and pray. Jesus found them sleeping and chided Peter, 'Couldn't you men keep watch with me for one hour? Watch and pray so that you will not fall into temptation. The spirit is willing, but the flesh is weak.' He went away a second and third time to pray the same prayer, only to return and find them sleeping again due to their exhaustion. After the third prayer, He woke them, saying, 'Are you still sleeping and resting? Look, the hour has come, and the Son of Man is delivered into the hands of sinners' (Matthew 26:40-45).

The events in the Garden of Gethsemane reached a dramatic climax with the arrival of Judas Iscariot, who led a crowd armed with swords and clubs, sent by the chief priests and elders. The betrayal, sealed with a kiss, marked the start of the series of events that led to His arrest and subsequent trial.

The Betrayal and Arrest

After spending time in prayer in the Garden of Gethsemane, Jesus faced one of the darkest moments of His life: the betrayal by one of His own disciples, Judas Iscariot. Judas, one of the Twelve, had arranged with the chief priests to betray Jesus in exchange for thirty pieces of silver. This act of betrayal was not a spur-of-the-moment decision but a deliberate choice that led to Jesus' arrest and ultimately His crucifixion.

The Gospels tell us that Judas led a crowd armed with swords and clubs, sent by the chief priests and the elders, to where Jesus and His disciples were. Judas had given them a sign, saying, 'The one I kiss is the man; arrest him' (Matthew 26:48). When Judas arrived, he approached Jesus, greeted Him, and kissed Him. Jesus' response to this betrayal was one of sorrow but also of acceptance, as He addressed Judas, 'Do what you came for, friend' (Matthew 26:50). In this moment, Jesus' use of the word 'friend' to address Judas is profound, reflecting His unwavering love and forgiveness, even in betrayal.

The arrest of Jesus followed immediately after Judas' betrayal. Despite being innocent of any crime, Jesus did not resist arrest. Instead, He questioned the need for the crowd to come out with swords and clubs as if He were a criminal. He highlighted the irony that He had been teaching openly in the temple courts daily, yet they chose to arrest Him under the cover of night.

The disciples' reaction to Jesus' arrest was marked by fear and confusion. In an attempt to defend Jesus, Peter drew his sword and struck the servant of the high priest, cutting off his ear. Jesus immediately rebuked Peter for his action, saying, 'Put your sword back in its place, for all who draw the sword will die by the sword. Do you think I cannot call on my Father, and He will at once put at my disposal more than twelve legions of angels? But how then would the Scriptures be fulfilled that say it must happen in this way?' (Matthew 26:52-54). Then Jesus healed the servant's ear. The servant's name was Malchus. This response underscores Jesus' commitment to fulfilling the Scriptures and His decision not to use His tremendous power for personal gain, even in the face of imminent suffering.

In the events surrounding Jesus' arrest in the Garden of Gethsemane, His divine nature was unmistakably displayed. Addressing His betrayer as a 'friend' and questioning the need for his arrestors to approach under cover of night, Jesus illuminated the hypocrisy of the religious leaders orchestrating His capture. Even more compelling was His healing of the servant's ear, demonstrating compassion in the face of betrayal and violence. His statement, 'those who live by the sword will die by the sword,' frequently cited in popular discourse, originates from Him and underscores a profound truth about the consequences of violence.

Furthermore, Jesus declared His ability to summon legions of angels for His defense yet chose restraint, emphasizing, 'for this moment have I come for the redemption of humanity.' This deliberate choice not to exercise His immense power, to allow the unfolding of events meant for human salvation, resonates as a powerful testament to His divinity and sacrificial love.

The Condemnation

After His arrest in the Garden of Gethsemane, Jesus was taken to the high priest, where the chief priests, the elders, and the teachers of the law had gathered. They were seeking evidence against Jesus to justify His execution, but they could not find any, despite many false witnesses coming forward. The high priest asked Jesus, "Are you the Messiah, the Son of the Blessed One?" Jesus replied, "Yes I am, and you will see the Son of Man sitting at the right hand of the Mighty One and coming on the clouds of heaven" (Mark 14:61-62), referring to the prophecy of Daniel about the Son of Man coming in the clouds of heaven. This statement provided the high priest and the council with the grounds to accuse Jesus of blasphemy, a charge that under their law was punishable by death.

It is important to recognize that the religious leaders' animosity towards Jesus was not a new development. Throughout His ministry, Jesus had repeatedly clashed with them over interpretations of the law, His challenges to their authority, and His radical teachings about love, forgiveness, and the kingdom of God. Actions such as healing on the Sabbath, associating with sinners, and claiming divine authority were seen as direct threats to the religious status quo. His increasing popularity only intensified the leaders' fear and envy.

The trial before the Sanhedrin, the ruling council, was riddled with legal irregularities: it took place at night, was hastily arranged, and relied on inconsistent testimonies. Nevertheless, the leaders' desire to remove Jesus as a threat to their power and their interpretation of the law took precedence over any commitment to justice. When Jesus affirmed His identity as the Messiah and mentioned His heavenly authority, the high priest accused Him of blasphemy and tore his clothes in a gesture that traditionally expressed mourning over a grievous sin.

The religious leaders' condemnation of Jesus was not just a rejection of a man but of His message of salvation, grace, and the coming of God's kingdom. Driven by fear, jealousy, and a profound misunderstanding of the scriptures, they failed to recognize the Messiah foretold by the prophets. In their zeal to preserve their religious traditions and authority, they unwittingly fulfilled God's plan for the sacrificial death of His Son, intended for the salvation of the world.

The Denial of Peter

The story unfolds during Jesus' arrest and subsequent trials. Peter had vowed his loyalty to Jesus hours earlier, asserting he would never abandon Him, even at the cost of his life. However, Jesus knew Peter better than Peter knew himself and predicted that he would deny Him three times before the rooster crowed (Matthew 26:34). Peter found the idea of betraying his Lord unimaginable.

Yet, as Jesus was taken for interrogation and beaten, fear and confusion overcame Peter. He followed Jesus at a distance to the high priest's courtyard, trying to remain inconspicuous. There, when servants and bystanders recognized him as a follower of Jesus, Peter's resolve wavered. Despite his earlier promises of steadfast loyalty, he denied knowing Jesus three times. His third denial coincided with the rooster's crow, fulfilling Jesus' prophecy. Immediately, Peter recalled Jesus' prediction of his denial. The realization of his betrayal, especially during Jesus' most dire moment, overwhelmed him. He broke down and wept bitterly (Matthew 26:75), a profound lesson in humility and the frailty of human resolve. This is how the Bible describes Peter's denial:

"Then seizing him [Jesus], they led him away and took him into the house of the high priest. Peter followed at a distance. And when some there had kindled a fire in the middle of the courtyard and had sat down together, Peter sat down with them. A servant girl saw him seated there in the firelight. She looked closely at him and said, "This man was with him." But he denied it. "Woman, I don't know him," he said. A little later someone else saw him and said, "You also are one of them." "Man, I am not!" Peter replied. About an hour later another asserted, "Certainly this fellow was with him, for he is a Galilean." Peter replied,

"Man, I don't know what you're talking about!" Just as he was speaking, the rooster crowed. The Lord turned and looked straight at Peter. Then Peter remembered the word the Lord had spoken to him: "Before the rooster crows today, you will disown me three times." And he went outside and wept bitterly" (Luke 22:54-62).

Peter's denial is crucial for several reasons. It highlights the vulnerability of even the most devoted followers. Despite his genuine love and intentions, Peter succumbed to fear and self-preservation, a warning to all believers about the potential for weakness, particularly under duress.

Moreover, this incident illuminates Jesus' understanding of human frailty and His readiness to forgive. Rather than rejecting Peter, Jesus, after His resurrection, reaffirmed His love and mission to Peter, entrusting him with the leadership of His followers (John 21:15-17). This act of forgiveness and restoration epitomizes Jesus' ministry, emphasizing redemption over condemnation.

Trial before Pilate

After being condemned by the religious leaders for blasphemy, Jesus was taken to Pilate early in the morning, as only the Roman authorities could carry out the death penalty. The chief priests and elders accused Jesus of claiming to be the king of the Jews and inciting rebellion against Rome. Aware of the religious leaders' envy and potential unrest, Pilate questioned Jesus, asking, "Are you the king of the Jews?" (Matthew 27:11). Jesus' reply, "You have said so," served both as an affirmation and a challenge, prompting Pilate to consider a form of kingship that transcended political power.

Caught in a web of political pressure, public opinion, and his own sense of justice, Pilate found no basis for a charge against Jesus but hesitated to release Him, fearing the crowd's reaction and potential backlash from Roman authorities. To appease the crowd, Pilate offered to release Jesus as part of a Passover amnesty, but this gesture backfired when the crowd, influenced by the chief priests, chose Barabbas, a known insurrectionist, over Jesus.

Pilate's interactions with Jesus and the crowd exposed his inner conflict and the broader issue of justice versus expediency. Pilate famously questioned, "What is truth?" (John 18:38), reflecting his personal skepticism and the philosophical and moral dilemmas faced by those in power. Standing before Pilate, Jesus personified the truth—truth about God, humanity, and the kingdom of heaven. Yet, Pilate, unable or unwilling to embrace this truth, chose political expediency over justice.

The trial before Pilate starkly contrasts the kingdom of God with the kingdoms of this world. Jesus, though innocent, accepted the injustice of human courts, fulfilling the Father's will and His mission of salvation. His demeanor under accusations, His patience during interrogation, and His acceptance of an unjust sentence demonstrate His profound love and the magnitude of His sacrifice.

Sent to Herod

After Jesus' initial trial before Pontius Pilate, the Roman governor faced a dilemma. Although he recognized that Jesus had not committed any crime worthy of death, he was under immense pressure from the religious leaders and the crowd who demanded Jesus' crucifixion. Discovering that Jesus was a Galilean and thus under Herod's jurisdiction, Pilate sent Jesus to Herod, who was in Jerusalem for the Passover festival (Luke 23:6-7). Herod Antipas, the son of Herod the Great and ruler over Galilee and Perea, was known for his lavish lifestyle and the infamous execution of John the Baptist. He plays a notable, though often overlooked, role in the events leading to Jesus' crucifixion.

Curious about Jesus, whom he had heard of through His teachings and miracles, Herod initially feared that Jesus was John the Baptist risen from the dead. When confronted with Jesus in person, Herod hoped to witness a miracle (Luke 23:8). However, Jesus remained silent, refusing to entertain or respond to him. Herod and his soldiers then mocked Jesus, dressing Him in an elegant robe to ridicule His claim to kingship, before sending Him back to Pilate (Luke 23:11). This encounter, marked by mockery and disrespect, underscored the contempt with which Jesus was treated by the political authorities.

The interaction between Pilate and Herod highlights the political maneuvering and evasion of responsibility in Jesus' trial. Although both rulers had the authority to release Jesus, they instead shuffled Him back and forth, succumbing to political pressures and the crowd's demands. Moreover, Herod's interest in Jesus was superficial, marked by a mocking desire to see a miracle, treating Jesus more as a spectacle than as the Son of God.

Notably, the Gospels mention that this event led to a reconciliation between Pilate and Herod, who had previously been at odds (Luke 23:12). This shared judgment of Jesus, albeit unjust, forged a bond between the two rulers. This detail underscores the irony and tragedy of human alliances formed through opposition to Jesus, reflecting the depths of human sinfulness and the perversion of justice.

Jesus' silence before Herod is profound, reflecting His sovereign choice not to defend Himself against false accusations or to perform signs on demand. His kingship and authority do not hinge on human acknowledgment or approval. His mission was not to impress through miracles but to save through sacrifice.

Sentenced to Death

After an inconclusive trial before Herod Antipas, Jesus was sent back to Pontius Pilate. This moment in the Passion narrative underscores the political and judicial indecision over Jesus' fate, revealing the reluctance of these rulers to make a definitive decision regarding His guilt or innocence. The return to Pilate marked the final phase of Jesus' trial, setting the stage for the events leading to His crucifixion.

Pilate found himself in a precarious position. He had already acknowledged Jesus' innocence, stating, "I find no basis for a charge against this man" (Luke 23:4). However, the chief priests, leaders, and the crowd were adamant in their demand for Jesus' execution. Pilate's initial attempt to defer the decision to Herod had failed to absolve him of responsibility, and with Jesus' return, he faced increasing pressure to appease the crowd and maintain order during the Passover festival.

Pilate had Jesus flogged, hoping this punishment would satisfy the crowd. However, the chief priests and the crowd persisted, demanding crucifixion and shouting, "Crucify him!" (Mark 15:13-14). In a final effort to release Jesus, Pilate presented Him to the crowd alongside Barabbas, a known insurrectionist and murderer. Pilate hoped that the crowd would choose Jesus, whom he considered harmless, over a known criminal. However, influenced by the chief priests and leaders, the crowd demanded Barabbas' release and Jesus' crucifixion. Pilate's question, "What crime has this man committed?" (Luke 23:22), was met with shouts of "Crucify him!" Pilate's decision to hand Jesus over for crucifixion was a tragic compromise, yielding to the mob's demands and renouncing his authority to do what was right.

Pilate's actions reflect the tension between justice and expediency. Despite his personal conviction of Jesus' innocence and his wife's warning about a troubling dream she had about Jesus, Pilate chose to satisfy the crowd's demands over executing fair judgment. In a symbolic act of washing his hands, Pilate declared himself innocent of Jesus' blood, effectively shifting the responsibility to the crowd, saying, "I am innocent of this man's blood... It is your responsibility!" (Matthew 27:24). Despite his claims of innocence, Pilate handed Jesus over to be flogged and then crucified, succumbing to the will of the people and the religious leaders.

The sentence of death by crucifixion was a brutal one, reserved for the worst criminals. Crucifixion was not only a form of execution but also a means of public humiliation and deterrence. Jesus, who had committed no crime and preached a message of love, forgiveness, and the coming of God's kingdom, was to suffer the most painful and humiliating death imaginable.

The sentencing of Jesus to death is a profound reminder of the depth of human sin and the lengths to which God was willing to go to restore the broken relationship between Himself and humanity. Jesus, fully God and fully man, submitted to this unjust sentence, demonstrating His obedience to the Father and His love for us. In doing so, He took upon Himself the penalty for our sins, offering us forgiveness and the promise of eternal life with God.

The Torture

The period following Jesus' condemnation to death and leading up to His journey to Calvary is among the most somber and heart-wrenching episodes in the Christian narrative. This time, marked by profound suffering and injustice, underscores the depth of Jesus' sacrifice for humanity. After Pontius Pilate handed Him over, Jesus endured severe torture at the hands of Roman soldiers, a painful prelude to the crucifixion that awaited Him.

The soldiers took Jesus into the palace known as the Praetorium and gathered the whole company around Him. They stripped Him and dressed Him in a purple robe, mocking Him as a king. They crafted a crown of thorns, placed it on His head, and began to salute Him, saying, "Hail, king of the Jews!" (Mark 15:16-18). This cruel irony, intended to demean and ridicule, only highlighted the stark contrast between the kingdom Jesus proclaimed and the worldly understanding of power and kingship.

Further, Jesus was struck on the head with a staff and spat upon, acts of physical and symbolic contempt (Mark 15:19). Beyond physical abuse, these actions aimed to degrade Jesus as profoundly as possible. After this mockery, they led Him out to crucify Him.

The torture inflicted on Jesus served multiple grim purposes in the Roman context: to deter would-be criminals, to demonstrate Roman authority, and to break the spirit of the condemned. Yet, in the divine narrative, Jesus' suffering takes on a transformative meaning. As prophesied by Isaiah, "He was oppressed and afflicted, yet he did not open his mouth; he was led like a lamb to the slaughter, and as a sheep before its shearers is silent, so he did not open his mouth" (Isaiah 53:7).

Jesus' silent endurance of suffering fulfilled this prophecy, highlighting His submission to God's will and His role as the sacrificial Lamb who takes away the sin of the world.

This intense period of torture, culminating in the crucifixion, underscores a central paradox of the Christian faith: through suffering and death comes life and salvation. Jesus' torture was not an end in itself but a passage to fulfill the divine purpose of redemption. He bore the physical and emotional scars of humanity's brokenness to offer healing and reconciliation with God. The account of Jesus' torture, while difficult to contemplate, is a crucial part of the Easter story. It underscores the cost of our freedom and the unsearchable riches of Christ's love for us—a love that endured the cross, scorned its shame, and emerged victorious in the resurrection, offering eternal life to all who believe.

The Crucifixion

After being sentenced to death by Pontius Pilate and subsequently tortured, Jesus carried the weight of the cross toward Calvary, also known as Golgotha, where He would be crucified, fulfilling the Scriptures that foretold the Messiah's suffering and death. It was customary for the condemned to carry their cross to the place of execution. Thus, Jesus began His painful journey to Golgotha, the place of the skull, burdened not just by the physical weight of the cross but by the weight of humanity's sins.

The path to Calvary was a Via Dolorosa, a way of suffering. Along this path, Simon of Cyrene was compelled by the Roman soldiers to carry the cross for Jesus, as His physical strength waned under the immense burden and the beatings He had endured. This act, while a momentary relief for Jesus, underscores the gravity of the moment and the physical reality of His suffering.

Crowds lined the way to Golgotha, some mourning and lamenting for Jesus. To the women who wept for Him, Jesus spoke, telling them not to weep for Him but for themselves and their children, prophesying the hardships that would come (Luke 23:28-31). Even in His suffering, Jesus' concern was for the welfare of others, highlighting His compassion and selflessness.

Upon arriving at Golgotha, Jesus was crucified between two criminals, fulfilling the prophecy that He would be 'numbered with the transgressors' (Isaiah 53:12). The inscription above His head, 'This is the King of the Jews,' intended to mock Him, spoke a profound truth about His kingship and the nature of His kingdom. Unlike earthly kings who lord their power over others, Jesus demonstrated His kingship through sacrifice and service.

Jesus' crucifixion at Calvary is where the sin of the world is confronted with the love and grace of God. It marks a turning point in human history, where love triumphed over hate, and life conquered death. Through His death, Jesus offered Himself as the perfect sacrifice for sin, fulfilling Old Testament prophecies and establishing a new covenant based on His blood. The crucifixion makes salvation and forgiveness of sins available to all who believe in Him.

AT THE CROSS

This section covers the following topics:

- *Introduction*
- *Forgiving the Persecutors*
- *Soldiers Casting Lots for His Clothes*
- *The Penitent Thief*
- *Jesus and His Mother*
- *Agony at the Cross*
- *It is Finished*
- *The Restoration*
- *The Death Certificate*
- *The Son of God Indeed*

Introduction

The events at the cross represent the pinnacle of Passion Week. Each moment after Jesus' crucifixion underscores a profound story of sacrifice and triumph, rooted deeply in emotional and theological layers. These last hours offer a glimpse into the dual nature of Christ—both fully human and fully divine.

As Jesus hung on the cross, He faced not only physical brutality but also spiritual burden. Condemned unjustly, He was tortured, mocked, and nailed to the cross, enduring extreme physical and emotional pain aimed at His destruction. Yet, in the midst of this agony, Jesus displayed unparalleled mercy, forgiving those who crucified Him. His forgiveness during such torment highlights the boundless depth of His love and His adherence to the principles He taught.

Amidst His suffering, soldiers gambled for His clothes beneath Him, fulfilling ancient prophecies and displaying a stark indifference to the sacred event unfolding. This act reveals the grim reality of human apathy in the face of divine sacrifice.

While crucified between two thieves, Jesus promised paradise to the repentant thief beside Him. This interaction underscores the vast reach of His grace, offering salvation even in the last moments of a man's life.

One of the most poignant scenes at the cross involved His mother, Mary. Despite His own suffering, Jesus ensured her future care, entrusting her to His disciple John. This act of filial piety amidst His own agony speaks volumes of His character and compassion.

The phrase "It is Finished" marked the conclusion of Jesus' earthly mission. With His final breath, He declared His work complete, achieving the redemption He came to bring. This proclamation not only signaled the end of His suffering but also the fulfillment of His mission to reconcile humanity with God.

At His death, the temple curtain tore, symbolically ending the separation between God and humanity and ushering in a new era of direct communion with the divine. This event signified the restoration of the relationship lost since Eden.

The certainty of Jesus' death was confirmed by a Roman soldier who pierced His side. This act was a necessary affirmation for those present, proving definitively that He had died—a crucial fact underscoring the reality of His sacrifice.

Ultimately, Jesus' divine nature was affirmed by those who witnessed these events, including a Roman centurion who recognized and proclaimed His deity. This acknowledgment by a likely skeptic highlights the undeniable impact of Jesus' death and the divine truth it represented.

As we dive into these moments at the cross, we reflect on their profound significance—not just as historical events, but as the cornerstone of Christian faith, exemplifying the ultimate demonstration of love and sacrifice.

Forgiving the Persecutors

In the midst of one of history's darkest hours, as Jesus hung on the cross, a profound and transformative act of forgiveness was displayed for all humanity. Amid His own agony, Jesus extended forgiveness to those who had orchestrated His suffering and crucifixion, uttering words that echo through the ages: "Father, forgive them, for they do not know what they are doing" (Luke 23:34). This plea for mercy on behalf of His persecutors is a cornerstone of Christian teaching, illustrating the boundless capacity for forgiveness that defines Jesus' message and mission.

This moment is striking for several reasons. First, it demonstrates Jesus' unwavering commitment to the principle of forgiveness, a theme central to His teachings throughout His ministry. Jesus had always taught His followers to love their enemies and pray for those who persecute them (Matthew 5:44), and even in the face of betrayal, false accusation, and physical torment, He lived out this command to the fullest extent.

Second, Jesus' act of forgiveness on the cross underscores the depth of His understanding and compassion. He recognized the blindness and ignorance of those who called for His death—their inability to see who He truly was or understand the significance of their actions. His plea to the Father was not just for the Roman soldiers who nailed Him to the cross, but for all who played a part in His prosecution, including the religious leaders and the crowds swayed by their influence. This recognition of human frailty and the propensity to act in ignorance is a poignant reminder of the need for forgiveness in our own lives.

THE LIFE OF CHRIST JESUS

Moreover, Jesus' forgiveness of His prosecutors points to the very heart of the gospel—the message of reconciliation. Through His death, Jesus provided the means for all humanity to be reconciled to God, forgiving our sins and bridging the gap that sin had created between God and humankind. This act of forgiveness on the cross is a vivid illustration of God's grace, offered freely to all, regardless of our offenses.

It also serves as a powerful testimony to the world about the nature of God's love—a love that forgives freely and fully, without reservation.

Soldiers Casting Lots for His Clothes

At the foot of the cross, as Jesus hung crucified, a seemingly small yet profoundly symbolic event took place—Roman soldiers cast lots for His clothes. This act is recorded in the Gospel of John, emphasizing its significance in the fulfillment of Scripture and the deep layers of meaning behind the crucifixion.

John 19:23-24 states, "When the soldiers crucified Jesus, they took his clothes, dividing them into four shares, one for each of them, with the undergarment remaining. This garment was seamless, woven in one piece from top to bottom. 'Let's not tear it,' they said to one another. 'Let's decide by lot who will get it.' This happened that the Scripture might be fulfilled which said, 'They divided my clothes among them and cast lots for my garment.' So this is what the soldiers did." These verses directly reference Psalm 22:18, where King David, centuries before Christ's birth, prophetically laments, "They divide my clothes among them and cast lots for my garment."

They were focused on dividing a small spoil, a mere piece of clothing, while above them, the salvation of humanity was being enacted. Furthermore, this scene at the foot of the cross depicts a stark irony. While Jesus was giving up His life as a ransom for many, providing spiritual liberation and eternal salvation, the soldiers were gambling over His earthly possessions. It highlights the spiritual blindness and the worldly focus that often characterize human nature, contrasting with the spiritual deliverance Jesus was achieving.

The Penitent Thief

Among the most compelling scenes at Calvary, where Jesus was crucified, is the interaction between Him and the two criminals crucified alongside Him. This narrative centers on one of them, often referred to as the penitent thief, who in his final moments turned to Jesus in faith and received the assurance of salvation. This episode, rich in mercy and grace, offers a profound insight into the nature of forgiveness and redemption.

As they hung on their crosses, the agony of crucifixion bearing down on them, the two criminals reacted to Jesus in markedly different ways. One hurled insults at Him, echoing the mockery of the bystanders, challenging Jesus to save Himself and them. However, the other criminal rebuked his companion, acknowledging their just punishment for crimes committed, contrasting their guilt with Jesus' innocence. He then turned to Jesus with a simple yet profound request: "Jesus, remember me when you come into your kingdom" (Luke 23:42).

This request from the penitent thief is remarkable for its faith and humility. In the midst of suffering and at the brink of death, he recognized Jesus as a king with a kingdom beyond this world. His plea for remembrance was not just a bid for mercy but an expression of belief in Jesus' power and authority, even as Jesus Himself was subjected to the cruel death of a criminal.

Jesus' response to the penitent thief is equally remarkable and reveals the heart of the Gospel: "Truly I tell you, today you will be with me in paradise" (Luke 23:43). With these words, Jesus offered the thief not only forgiveness but also the promise of eternal life with Him. This interaction is significant as it illustrates the first act of pardon and the offering of paradise following Jesus' sacrifice as the Lamb of God. It underscores that salvation is not earned by deeds but is a gift of grace to those who have faith in Jesus Christ.

The story of the penitent thief highlights several key aspects of Christian faith. First, it demonstrates that it is never too late to turn to Jesus. The thief's last-minute plea for mercy was met with open arms, reminding us of the boundless scope of God's grace. Second, this narrative reaffirms the power of sincere faith. Despite his past, the thief's recognition of Jesus as Lord at the moment of death was enough to secure his place in paradise. The Penitent Thief is a poignant reminder of the essence of the Easter message: redemption and new life are available to all through Jesus Christ, regardless of one's past.

Jesus and His Mother

Amidst the profound agony of the crucifixion, a deeply human and tender moment unfolded that illustrates the compassion and foresight of Jesus Christ. This moment, captured succinctly in the Gospel of John, involves Jesus entrusting the care of His mother, Mary, to His beloved disciple, John. This act is more than a simple provision for a loved one; it carries significant theological and spiritual implications.

John 19:26-27 recounts this poignant interaction: 'When Jesus saw his mother there, and the disciple whom he loved standing nearby, he said to her, 'Woman, here is your son,' and to the disciple, 'Here is your mother.' From that time on, this disciple took her into his home.' This scene is rich with meaning, showcasing Jesus' unwavering concern for the welfare of His mother even as He endured unimaginable suffering.

First and foremost, this act of entrusting His mother to John highlights the personal nature of Jesus' ministry. It reveals His human concern for the well-being of His loved ones, reflecting a profound sense of duty and care. Even in His final moments, Jesus fulfilled His responsibilities as a son, ensuring that His mother would be cared for after His death.

At this juncture, I must address a controversial issue regarding Jesus addressing His mother as 'woman.' Jesus called his mother 'woman' on two distinct occasions. The first instance occurred during the wedding at Cana (John 2:4), and the second was at the crucifixion (John 19:26). To appreciate the full significance behind Jesus calling his mother 'woman,' we need to consider its cultural, theological, and symbolic implications.

The first key to understanding Jesus' use of the term 'woman' is to consider the cultural context in which he lived. In ancient Israel, the word 'woman' was not considered disrespectful or derogatory. Rather, it was a respectful and socially acceptable form of address, similar to 'ma'am' or 'madam' in modern times. Recognizing this historical context allows us to appreciate that Jesus was not demeaning his mother by calling her 'woman' but addressing her with respect and courtesy.

In addition to its cultural context, the term 'woman' carries significant theological symbolism. In the Bible, Eve is the first woman, created from Adam's rib, and represents the beginning of humanity. However, Eve's disobedience led to the introduction of sin and death into the world. Conversely, Mary is often referred to as the 'new Eve' because her obedience to God brought forth Jesus, the Savior, and offered humanity the hope of redemption. By calling his mother, Mary, 'woman,' Jesus was likely drawing attention to her vital role in salvation history, emphasizing her importance not just as his own mother, but as a figure of paramount significance in the broader narrative of God's relationship with humanity.

"Jesus' use of the term "woman" can be seen as an affirmation of Mary's intercessory role. For instance, at the wedding in Cana, Mary brings the lack of wine to Jesus' attention. His response, "Woman, what does this have to do with me? My hour has not yet come," seems somewhat abrupt. However, despite stating that his time had not come, Jesus goes on to perform his first miracle by turning water into wine. This event demonstrates Mary's unique intercessory role, as she brings human needs to her son's notice and serves as an advocate for those in need.

During Jesus' crucifixion, he once again refers to his mother as "woman" while entrusting her to his beloved disciple John. In this heartrending moment, Jesus employs both the terms "woman" and "mother." By calling her "mother," Jesus ensures that Mary will be taken care of in her earthly life, acknowledging her maternal relationship with him.

THE LIFE OF CHRIST JESUS

Simultaneously, by addressing her as "woman," he highlights her spiritual role as the mother of all believers. This profound exchange underscores Mary's all-encompassing maternal role, which transcends her biological connection to Jesus and embraces everyone who follows him.

In examining the instances where Jesus called his mother, Mary, "woman" and the themes surrounding these events, we gain insight into the rich meaning behind this form of address. From his first miracle at the wedding in Cana to the heartrending moment at the cross, Jesus acknowledges and emphasizes Mary's intercessory role and her position as the spiritual mother of all believers. By understanding the context and significance of these events, we deepen our appreciation of Mary's vital role in the Christian faith, salvation history, and her enduring presence in the lives of believers throughout history.

It is possible that some readers will agree with my explanation, while others may reject it. Whether one is Catholic or Protestant, the theological implications of Mary's role can be viewed differently. However, it is essential to recognize that if Jesus is acknowledged as God, then, logically, Mary is the mother of God, or Theotokos, meaning 'God Bearer,' as we have seen in the chapter ' The Census and the Journey to Bethlehem'. It is crucial not to distort this fact or to selectively use Bible verses that might mislead other believers.

Agony at the Cross

In the agonizing final moments on the cross, recorded starkly in the Gospel of John, Jesus utters a statement loaded with physical and spiritual significance: 'I am thirsty' (John 19:28). This brief declaration, made during the crucifixion, reveals the profound humanity of Jesus Christ and deepens our understanding of His suffering.

As He hung on the cross, the physical toll on Jesus was extreme. The loss of blood, combined with dehydration under the torturous conditions of crucifixion, led to His intense physical thirst. Following Jesus' expression of thirst, the soldiers offered Him vinegar to drink, using a sponge lifted on a hyssop branch. This act, while appearing to be a minor detail, is rich with biblical symbolism. It fulfilled the prophecy found in Psalm 69:21, which states, 'They put gall in my food and gave me vinegar for my thirst.' The hyssop plant was used for purification and sacrificial rituals in the Old Testament, symbolizing the purification from sin that Jesus' sacrifice offers to humanity.

Amid the harrowing hours on the cross, one of the most profound utterances by Jesus is His cry, 'My God, my God, why have you forsaken me?' (Matthew 27:46 and Mark 15:34). This poignant expression of anguish highlights Jesus' suffering and is a direct quotation from Psalm 22:1, a psalm that vividly describes suffering and deliverance. By invoking these words, Jesus fulfills the scriptures and aligns His experience with the prophetic writings that foretell the Messiah's ordeals. Psalm 22, while starting in despair, ends in triumph and affirmation of God's sovereignty, mirroring the trajectory of Jesus' own path from crucifixion to resurrection.

THE LIFE OF CHRIST JESUS

Jesus' plea is often misunderstood as a moment of doubt or loss of faith. However, it is important to recognize the depth of His human experience at that moment—feeling the weight of the world's sins and the separation from God that sin causes. In bearing the sins of humanity, Jesus experienced a profound sense of alienation from God, something He had never known before, making this expression one of the most relatable moments of His earthly ministry. This forsakenness was necessary for the atonement of humanity's sins. Through His death, Jesus bridged the chasm sin created between God and man, offering reconciliation and a path back to spiritual intimacy with the Father.

It is Finished

In the climactic moments on the cross, Jesus uttered three words that encapsulate the culmination of His earthly mission: 'It is finished' (John 19:30). This profound declaration, spoken with His last breaths, marks not only the end of His physical suffering but also the completion of a divine plan set in motion from the foundation of the world. These words carry weighty significance, reflecting the fulfillment of prophecy, the accomplishment of redemption, and the victory over sin and death.

As Jesus hung on the cross, He endured unimaginable suffering. After His cry of abandonment, 'My God, my God, why have you forsaken me?' (Matthew 27:46), His declaration of 'It is finished' signals a triumphant conclusion to the work He was sent to accomplish.

The phrase 'It is finished' signifies the completion of the sacrificial system that defined the Old Covenant. Jesus, the perfect Lamb of God, offered Himself as the ultimate sacrifice, once and for all, fulfilling the law and the prophets. This act of selfless love satisfied the just requirements of a holy God, bridging the gap between the Creator and His creation. Through His death, Jesus provided the means for humanity's reconciliation with God, making a way for us to be forgiven and restored to a right relationship with Him.

Furthermore, Jesus' words underscore the defeat of the powers of darkness. By willingly laying down His life, Jesus disarmed the principalities and powers, triumphing over them through the cross (Colossians 2:15). His death, far from being a defeat, was the decisive blow in the cosmic battle between good and evil, securing victory for all who would put their trust in Him. The debt of sin has been paid in full;

THE LIFE OF CHRIST JESUS

nothing more can or needs to be added to what Jesus accomplished on the cross. This truth brings immense freedom and peace, allowing believers to live in the joy and assurance of their salvation.

However, it is crucial to address a common misinterpretation of Jesus' sacrifice that some may espouse. While Jesus indeed paid the ultimate price for sin, this should not be misconstrued as a license for moral laxity. Some may wrongly suggest, under the guise of prosperity theology or a reluctance to preach on sin and repentance, that since Jesus has paid for past, present, and future sins, one can live without moral restraint. This distortion of the gospel not only undermines the seriousness of sin but also contradicts the teachings of the New Testament, which calls for a life of repentance and holiness in response to God's grace (Romans 6:1-2). What Jesus accomplished on the cross was the final and complete sacrifice, eliminating the need for the Old Testament system of animal sacrifices and establishing a new covenant based on faith and repentance. It is not a carte blanche to sin but an invitation to live a life worthy of the sacrifice made, a life transformed by gratitude and guided by the Holy Spirit.

'It is Finished' is not merely the conclusion of Jesus' earthly life but the beginning of a new creation for all who believe in Him. It marks the dawn of hope, the assurance of forgiveness, and the promise of eternal life.

At the moment of Jesus' death, the natural world bore witness in a remarkable display, underscoring the profound significance of what had occurred. As narrated in the Gospel of Matthew, 'And when Jesus had cried out again in a loud voice, he gave up his spirit. At that moment the curtain of the temple was torn in two from top to bottom. The earth shook, the rocks split, and the tombs broke open' (Matthew 27:50-52).

This powerful description captures not just a physical event but a cosmic reaction to the death of the Son of God. Recall that when Jesus was born the sky lit up. When He died, the earth shook. The earthquake and the splitting rocks can be seen as creation mourning its Creator.

The Restoration

The moment Jesus uttered His final breath and declared, 'It is finished,' an extraordinary event occurred that symbolized the restoration of a broken relationship between God and humanity. The curtain in the temple, a thick and ornate veil that separated the Holy of Holies—the earthly dwelling place of God's presence—from the rest of the temple, was torn in two from top to bottom (Matthew 27:51). This act, far from incidental, carried deep theological significance, marking the fulfillment of God's plan for redemption and the removal of barriers that sin had erected.

To understand the full impact of the tearing of the veil, one must journey back to the Garden of Eden. When Adam and Eve sinned, their disobedience introduced sin into the world, creating a barrier between humanity and God. This separation was not only spiritual but represented in the physical layout of the temple, where the Holy of Holies was accessible only once a year by the high priest, and then only with a blood sacrifice for the sins of the people (Leviticus 16). The veil itself symbolized this profound separation, a constant reminder of the chasm sin had created.

The tearing of the veil at the moment of Jesus' death was a divine act, signifying the end of the old covenant and the establishment of a new one. This was God Himself removing the barrier, making it clear that access to His presence was no longer limited to a select few or mediated by animal sacrifices. Jesus, through His sacrificial death, had become the ultimate and final offering for sin, fulfilling what the sacrifices of the Old Testament could only point towards.

The writer of Hebrews eloquently speaks to this new access granted through Jesus: 'Therefore, brothers and sisters, since we have confidence to enter the Most Holy Place by the blood of Jesus, by a new and living way opened for us through the curtain, that is, his body' (Hebrews 10:19-20). Jesus' body, broken for us, is the new veil through which we gain direct access to God. This access is not just for the religious elite or those of a certain lineage but is available to all who believe in Jesus, tearing down the walls of separation and inviting us into a personal and intimate relationship with God.

It represents not only the re-establishment of a relationship lost in Eden but also the fulfillment of God's promise to dwell among His people. In Jesus, God came to live among us, share in our sufferings, and ultimately, through His death, bridge the gap that sin had created. The torn veil is a powerful symbol of Jesus' role as our High Priest, who intercedes on our behalf and through whom we can approach God with boldness and confidence.

The Death Certificate

After Jesus declared "It is finished" and bowed His head, giving up His spirit, the Roman authorities needed to ensure He was truly dead, a standard procedure to prevent any chance of survival or escape. John 19:33-34 vividly recounts this moment: "But when they came to Jesus and found that he was already dead, they did not break his legs. Instead, one of the soldiers pierced Jesus' side with a spear, bringing a sudden flow of blood and water." This act was not merely a methodical confirmation of death but also carried deep spiritual significance.

The flow of blood and water from Jesus' side is rich in symbolic meaning. Theologically, the blood represents the life-giving sacrifice of Jesus, shedding His blood for the remission of sins, aligning with the sacrifices of the Old Testament but fulfilling them in a new and everlasting covenant. The water symbolizes purification, echoing the cleansing rites of the Old Testament and pointing towards baptism, a foundational sacrament in Christianity that signifies new life and cleansing from sin.

This event also fulfilled the prophecy found in Zechariah 12:10, "They will look on me, the one they have pierced," and underscores the scriptural depth of the New Testament writers' claims. John's inclusion of this detail highlights the precision of Old Testament prophecies and their fulfillment in the life and death of Jesus, reinforcing His messianic identity and the divine orchestration of His mission.

Now, I must address a controversy that has persisted over the centuries: the claim that Jesus did not actually die on the cross. Some skeptics argue that Jesus merely fainted and later revived in the tomb. Additionally, according to Islamic belief, Jesus was not crucified at all;

instead, they assert that someone else was made to look like Him and was crucified in His place.

Let us first consider the nature of Roman crucifixion. This method of execution was meticulously designed to inflict maximum pain and ensure death. The process was not only excruciating but also methodically brutal. Victims of crucifixion were nailed to a cross, and death usually occurred through a combination of factors such as shock, blood loss, dehydration, and asphyxiation. To leave no doubt about the death of the crucified, Roman soldiers would often break the legs of the condemned, hastening death by preventing them from pushing up to breathe. This practice was a grim assurance that no one could survive crucifixion.

In the case of Jesus, the Roman soldiers did not break His legs because He was already dead. Instead, one soldier pierced His side with a spear, bringing forth a sudden flow of blood and water—a clear sign of death, as described in the Gospel of John (John 19:34). This action by the Roman soldier inadvertently served as a de facto death certificate. It is implausible to suggest that a person could endure such severe trauma and still be alive.

Addressing the Islamic claim that someone else was substituted for Jesus, we must consider the historical and eyewitness evidence. The Gospels consistently affirm that it was Jesus Himself who was crucified. His mother, His disciples, and many others who knew Him personally witnessed His crucifixion. These accounts were written and circulated within the lifetime of those witnesses, leaving little room for such a dramatic and deceptive substitution to go unnoticed or unchallenged.

Any fair examination of the historical and medical evidence, coupled with the consistency of eyewitness testimonies, leads to the inescapable conclusion that Jesus Christ indeed died on the cross. This death was not only real but necessary for the fulfillment of His mission as the Son

THE LIFE OF CHRIST JESUS

of God. As we will explore in the next chapter, the declaration by the Roman centurion that Jesus is the Son of God serves as further proof that it was indeed Jesus who was crucified, affirming His divine nature and the hope of eternal life for all who believe.

The Son of God Indeed

In the climactic moments of Jesus' crucifixion, an extraordinary shift occurred in the hearts and minds of some who had previously mocked and scorned Him. Amidst the darkness that fell over the land and the earth-shaking events that followed Jesus' final breath, a profound realization dawned upon those who witnessed His suffering: Jesus was not a criminal deserving death but the Son of God indeed. This acknowledgment, coming from unlikely sources, marks a pivotal moment in the narrative of the crucifixion, highlighting the divine identity of Jesus and the transformative power of His death.

As Jesus hung on the cross, the soldiers gambled for His clothes, and the passersby hurled insults at Him. The religious leaders mocked Him, challenging Him to save Himself and come down from the cross if He truly was the Messiah. Even one of the criminals crucified beside Him joined in the derision. However, as the events unfolded, the atmosphere began to change. Darkness covered the land for three hours, a supernatural occurrence that signaled the gravity of the moment (Luke 23:44-45).

After Jesus cried out and gave up His spirit, the curtain of the temple was torn in two from top to bottom, an act signifying the removal of the barrier between God and humanity (Matthew 27:51). This, coupled with the earthquake and the breaking open of the tombs, was undeniable evidence of the momentous nature of Jesus' death. It was in this context that the centurion and those with him who were guarding Jesus witnessed the earthquake and all that had happened. They were terrified and exclaimed, "Surely he was the Son of God!" (Matthew 27:54).

THE LIFE OF CHRIST JESUS

The centurion's declaration is particularly striking. As a Roman soldier, he would have been accustomed to crucifixions and unlikely to be moved by the suffering of a condemned man. However, the extraordinary circumstances surrounding Jesus' death—the darkness, the earthquake, the rending of the temple curtain—led him to a profound acknowledgment of Jesus' true nature. This confession, from a Gentile and a representative of Roman authority, underscores the universal significance of Jesus' death and His identity as the Savior, not just for the elites but for all humanity.

This moment of recognition serves multiple purposes within the Christian faith. First, it confirms the identity of Jesus as the Son of God, vindicating Him in the face of false accusations and mockery. Second, it illustrates the reach of Jesus' sacrificial death, extending grace and the possibility of faith to all, including those who were complicit in His crucifixion. Lastly, it showcases the power of God to reveal truth in the most unlikely circumstances, opening the eyes of witnesses to acknowledge the divine nature of Jesus.

THE RESURRECTION AND ASCENSION

This section covers the following topics:

- *Introduction*
- *In the Tomb*
- *Defeating Death*
- *The Appearances*
- *The Greatest Skeptic Ever Lived*
- *Barbecue at the Beach*
- *Choosing a Successor*
- *The Great Commission*
- *The Good Bye*
- *The Promise of the Second Coming*
- *Establishing His Identity*
- *Epilogue: The Journey Continues*

Introduction

The Resurrection and Ascension of Jesus Christ are cornerstone events that define Christianity, showcasing God's power over death and His plan for eternal salvation. This section explores these miraculous events, each step reaffirming the deity of Christ and the truth of His teachings, thereby strengthening the foundation of Christian faith.

The narrative begins with a somber moment as Jesus is laid in the tomb. Though filled with sorrow, this act sets the stage for the glory of the Resurrection. The sealed and guarded tomb, meant to end the story of Jesus, instead becomes the backdrop for its most triumphant chapter. When Jesus rises from the dead, He not only fulfills His own predictions and the prophecies about Him but also demonstrates His power over death, confirming His identity as the Son of God.

The Resurrection is more than an event; it is a testament to the reality of Jesus' promises. His appearances to the disciples and others serve to solidify the truth of His resurrection. These encounters, described in various settings—from the road to Emmaus to the shores of the Sea of Galilee—are intimate and transformative, designed to reassure His followers and equip them for the mission ahead.

Particularly compelling is the incident involving Thomas, famously dubbed "Doubting Thomas." His initial skepticism and subsequent belief upon touching Jesus' wounds provide a powerful narrative on faith, evidence, and personal transformation. Jesus' gentle rebuke and invitation to believe without seeing are profound lessons for all believers about the nature of faith and the reliability of Jesus' word.

One of the most poignant appearances occurs by the Sea of Galilee on the beach, where Jesus, after His resurrection, organizes a barbecue with His disciples. This moment emphasizes His continued fellowship with them, reinforcing His teachings and preparing them for their future without His physical presence. It is here that Jesus also reaffirms Peter's role, appointing him as a key leader. This act of passing the mantle to Peter signifies the continuity of His church and mission.

The Ascension of Jesus is the final act in this divine drama, where He rises into heaven in the sight of His disciples. This event not only marks the end of His earthly ministry but also signifies the beginning of His heavenly reign and the coming of the Holy Spirit, who would empower the apostles. The Ascension reinforces the promise of Jesus' omnipresence and His ongoing intercession for believers at the right hand of the Father.

Lastly, the promise of the Second Coming keeps the hope of His return alive in the hearts of believers. This future event is anticipated as the ultimate fulfillment of God's plan, where Christ will return to judge and restore all things, offering eternal life and unending joy to those who have believed in Him.

Together, these segments of The Resurrection and Ascension not only validate the historical claims of Christianity but also offer an enduring hope based on the tangible reality of Jesus' life, death, and resurrection. They challenge believers to live in the light of these truths and encourage a steadfast, hopeful anticipation of Christ's promised return.

In the Tomb

In the quiet aftermath of the crucifixion, as the noise of the crowd faded and the sky cleared, a profound act of devotion and respect took place. Jesus was laid in the tomb, marking a moment of sorrow and reflection for His followers. This event, though shrouded in grief, was a crucial part of the Easter story, setting the stage for the miracle of the resurrection.

After Jesus breathed His last on the cross, Joseph of Arimathea, a secret disciple of Jesus for fear of the religious leaders, stepped forward. He went to Pilate and asked for Jesus' body. Pilate, surprised to hear that Jesus was already dead, summoned the centurion to confirm His death before releasing the body to Joseph (Mark 15:43-45). Joseph's request was an act of courage and loyalty, revealing his deep respect for Jesus even in death.

Joseph, along with Nicodemus, who earlier had visited Jesus by night to inquire about His teachings, took Jesus' body down from the cross. They wrapped it in linen cloths with spices, as was the burial custom (John 19:39-40). This preparation of the body was a final act of service and care, a tribute to the man they revered as teacher and Lord.

The tomb where Jesus was laid was new, hewn out of rock, and belonged to Joseph of Arimathea. This fulfilled the prophecy that He would be buried with the rich (Isaiah 53:9). The body was placed in the tomb, and a large stone was rolled against the entrance, sealing it shut. Mary Magdalene and the other Mary sat opposite the tomb, silent witnesses to these solemn events.

The sealing of the tomb was not the end but a pause before the dawn of the most glorious day in Christian faith—the resurrection. Yet, in that moment of burial, all seemed lost. The disciples were scattered, fear and confusion reigned, and the hope that Jesus had ignited in the hearts of many appeared to be extinguished.

The burial of Jesus serves as a powerful reminder of the reality of death and the cost of redemption. It underscores the humanity of Jesus, who experienced death just as we do. Yet, even in the tomb, God's plan was at work, and the power of God was about to be dramatically revealed. The tomb, a place of darkness and despair, would soon become the site of the greatest victory—over sin and death.

Defeating Death

The resurrection of Jesus Christ is the most miraculous and significant event in history, marking the moment when Jesus defeated death and proclaimed victory over sin. This event, filled with supernatural occurrences and divine intervention, unfolded early in the morning on the first day of the week, forever changing the course of human history and the lives of those who believe in Him.

Before dawn, the earth itself bore witness to the magnitude of what was about to occur. An earthquake shook the ground as an angel of the Lord descended from heaven. This was no ordinary tremor nor an ordinary angel; the earth shook as the power of God intervened in the natural order, signaling the defeat of death and the dawning of a new creation (Matthew 28:2). The angel, whose appearance was like lightning and whose clothes were as white as snow, came down with a specific purpose—to roll back the stone that sealed Jesus' tomb. This act was not to let Jesus out, for He had already risen, but to reveal to the world that the tomb was empty.

The guards stationed at the tomb to prevent any tampering were struck with terror at the sight of the angel. Their fear was so intense that they shook and became like dead men (Matthew 28:4). These trained soldiers, representatives of Rome's power and authority, were powerless in the presence of God's messenger, highlighting the supremacy of divine power over human might.

As dawn approached, Mary Magdalene and the other Mary came to the tomb, carrying spices to anoint Jesus' body as per the custom. Their journey was marked by devotion but also by despair, as they mourned the loss of their Lord. However, what they found at the tomb was beyond their comprehension.

The stone had been rolled away, and an angel greeted them with words that would transform their sorrow into joy: "Do not be afraid, for I know that you are looking for Jesus, who was crucified. He is not here; he has risen, just as he said. Come and see the place where he lay" (Matthew 28:5-6). This invitation to witness the empty tomb was also a call to remember Jesus' words, to recall His promise of resurrection.

The angel then instructed the women to go quickly and tell the disciples that Jesus had risen from the dead and that He was going ahead of them into Galilee, where they would see Him. This message, though filled with hope, was also a commission—a call to be witnesses of the resurrection (Matthew 28:7). The women, filled with fear and great joy, ran to deliver the angel's message, becoming the first evangelists of the risen Christ.

Upon hearing the astonishing news from Mary Magdalene that the tomb was empty, some of the disciples were compelled to see for themselves. Peter and John, in particular, rushed to the tomb, driven by a mixture of hope and skepticism. When they arrived, they found the tomb exactly as Mary had described: empty, with the stone rolled away. Inside, the linen cloths that had wrapped Jesus' body lay there, a silent testament to the miraculous event that had occurred. John, upon seeing the empty tomb and the discarded linens, believed in the resurrection, even though he did not yet fully understand the Scripture that Jesus must rise from the dead (John 20:3-9).

The resurrection of Jesus is not just an event to be celebrated; it is the foundation of Christian faith. It declares that death has been defeated, that sin's power is broken, and that eternal life is available to all who believe in Him.

The Appearances

After the resurrection of Jesus, a series of remarkable appearances to His disciples and others unfolded, each encounter serving to strengthen their faith, commission them for the work ahead, and affirm the reality of His victory over death. These appearances are not just accounts of joyous reunions but pivotal moments that underscore the truth of the resurrection and its implications for believers.

One of the first appearances of the risen Jesus was to Mary Magdalene, outside the tomb. Overcome with sorrow and assuming Jesus' body had been taken away, she did not recognize Him until He called her by name (John 20:16). Mary's subsequent rush to tell the disciples, "I have seen the Lord!" (John 20:18), marks the first proclamation of the resurrected Christ, setting a pattern for witness that continues to this day.

On that same day, Jesus appeared to two followers on the road to Emmaus. These disciples, walking and discussing the recent events surrounding Jesus' crucifixion, were joined by a stranger who explained to them the scriptures concerning the Messiah. Despite their initial inability to recognize Him, their eyes were opened to His identity when He broke bread with them: "When he was at the table with them, he took bread, gave thanks, broke it and began to give it to them. Then their eyes were opened and they recognized him, and he disappeared from their sight" (Luke 24:30-31).

This revelation not only restored their hope but also emphasized the importance of fellowship and the breaking of bread in recognizing Jesus' presence among us. The moment of breaking bread with Jesus was a profound spiritual awakening for the disciples, highlighting the significance of communal acts in experiencing and understanding His presence. Filled with renewed faith and excitement, the two disciples hurried back to Jerusalem to share the news with the others, reinforcing the theme of witness and testimony that characterizes all of Jesus' post-resurrection appearances.

Perhaps one of the most well-known appearances occurred when Jesus came to His disciples as they were gathered behind locked doors for fear of the religious leaders. Jesus stood among them and said, "Peace be with you!" (John 20:19). He showed them His hands and side, providing tangible proof of His resurrection and dispelling their fears with His peace. This appearance was crucial in transforming the disciples from a group paralyzed by fear into bold witnesses of the resurrection.

A week later, Jesus appeared again to the disciples, this time including Thomas, who had doubted the reports of Jesus' resurrection. Jesus invited Thomas to touch His wounds, leading Thomas to proclaim, "My Lord and my God!" (John 20:28). This encounter addresses the reality of doubt within faith, showing that Jesus is willing to meet us in our skepticism and lead us to a place of belief. I address this further in the next chapter.

Another significant appearance occurred by the Sea of Galilee, where Jesus prepared breakfast for the disciples. Here, He reinstated Peter, who had denied Him three times before the crucifixion, asking Peter three times if he loved Him and commissioning him to "Feed my sheep" (John 21:17). This act of forgiveness and recommissioning underscores the theme of restoration and the calling of the disciples to continue Jesus's work. I further address this under chapters 'Barbecue at the Beach' and 'Choosing a Successor'.

These appearances of Jesus after His resurrection were foundational for the early Christian community, affirming the truth of the resurrection and empowering the disciples for the mission ahead. They serve as a testament to the reality of Jesus' victory over death and His ongoing presence with His followers.

The Greatest Skeptic Ever Lived

When it comes to the resurrection of Jesus, skepticism has always been a common response. Throughout history and even today, many self-proclaimed skeptics demand proof, often reveling in their perceived intellectual superiority as they pose questions that are frequently nothing more than straw man arguments. However, there was one skeptic who stood above the rest—someone who demanded the most compelling evidence of all. This individual was none other than Thomas, famously known as 'Doubting Thomas.' No other skeptic in history has so fully embodied that adjective. Let us explore the powerful story of how Jesus responded to Thomas' doubt and how Thomas reacted upon seeing the undeniable proof of the resurrection.

After Jesus' crucifixion and reported resurrection, the disciples were engulfed in a whirlwind of fear, confusion, and awe. Jesus appeared to them, offering peace and showing His wounds as proof of His resurrection. However, Thomas was not present during this appearance, and upon hearing the account from the other disciples, he expressed profound skepticism. He famously declared, "Unless I see the nail marks in his hands and put my finger where the nails were, and put my hand into his side, I will not believe" (John 20:25). Thomas' demand for physical evidence of the resurrection highlights a very human need for tangible proof in the face of extraordinary claims.

A week later, Jesus appeared again to His disciples, this time with Thomas present. Aware of Thomas' doubts, Jesus directly addressed him, offering His wounds as evidence and inviting Thomas to touch them and believe. In this moment, Jesus did not rebuke Thomas for his skepticism but met him where he was, providing the proof he needed to overcome his doubts. Jesus said to Thomas, "Put your finger here;

see my hands. Reach out your hand and put it into my side. Stop doubting and believe." Thomas' response, "My Lord and my God!" (John 20:26-28), marks one of the clearest confessions of faith in the New Testament, a declaration of Jesus' divinity and the truth of His resurrection.

This encounter between Jesus and Thomas is profoundly significant for several reasons. First, it demonstrates Jesus' understanding and compassion towards those who struggle with doubt. Jesus' willingness to provide evidence of His resurrection underscores His desire for all to come to faith, even those who, like Thomas, require more than testimonies to believe.

Second, the story of Thomas serves as powerful evidence of the reality of the resurrection. The physicality of Jesus' resurrected body, able to be seen and touched, leaves no trace of doubt about the truth of His victory over death. This tangible proof of the resurrection provided to Thomas (and, by extension, to all believers through his story) fortifies the Christian faith against skepticism, offering a solid foundation upon which to build our belief.

Furthermore, Jesus' words to Thomas, "Because you have seen me, you have believed; blessed are those who have not seen and yet have believed" (John 20:29), extend a blessing to future generations of believers. This pronouncement acknowledges the faith of those who believe in the resurrection without the benefit of physical proof, highlighting the blessedness of faith that trusts in the testimony of the Scriptures and the witness of the Holy Spirit.

The account of Thomas' transition from doubt to faith is an invitation to all who wrestle with questions and uncertainties about the Christian faith. It reassures us that Jesus is patient with our doubts, willing to meet us in our skepticism, and able to provide the assurance we need to believe. It challenges us to move beyond doubt to a place of faith and worship, recognizing Jesus for who He truly is: our Lord and our God.

In reflecting on the story of Doubting Thomas, we are reminded that the Christian faith is not a call to blind belief but a belief grounded in the historical reality of the resurrection, attested by eyewitnesses and validated by Jesus' interactions with His disciples. Thomas' story, far from being a tale of rebuke, is a narrative of grace, inviting all who doubt to encounter the risen Christ and, in doing so, to leave no trace of doubt behind.

So, if you are a skeptic, the question I pose to you is this: "Do you truly seek answers, or are you content with merely asking questions without a genuine desire for resolution?" If it is the latter, then no one can help you. But if it is the former, know that Jesus Himself has provided the answer: "Stop doubting and believe. Blessed are those who have not seen and yet have believed" (John 20:29). This blessing is not reserved solely for Christians; it is open to all, including skeptics and non-Christians. Embrace the invitation to believe, and you too can experience the profound blessing that faith brings.

Barbecue at the Beach

Jesus appeared to His disciples in several profound and intimate ways. One such encounter, which I call "Barbecue at the Beach," took place by the Sea of Galilee. This gathering was not only a testament to the risen Christ but also a reaffirmation of His relationship with His disciples, a moment filled with teaching, restoration, and fellowship.

After a night of fruitless fishing, the disciples were called to shore by a figure who turned out to be the resurrected Jesus, though they did not recognize Him immediately. He instructed them to cast their net on the right side of the boat, leading to an abundant catch, a miracle that mirrored an earlier one in their ministry (Luke 5:1-11) and helped them recognize Him. "It is the Lord!" John exclaimed (John 21:7). This recognition sparked a rush of joy and awe, especially for Peter, who jumped into the water to reach Jesus more quickly.

Once on shore, they found Jesus had prepared a charcoal fire with fish and bread, inviting them to bring some of their freshly caught fish and join Him for breakfast. This simple meal by the sea was more than a gathering; it was a sacramental moment that bridged the gap between the ordinary and the divine. Jesus, in His resurrected body, chose to spend time eating with His disciples, underscoring the continuity of His relationship with them despite the profound changes His death and resurrection had introduced.

During this meal, Jesus turned to Peter, offering him an opportunity for restoration. After Peter's denial before the crucifixion, this moment by the sea provided a path back to fellowship and leadership within the group. Jesus asked Peter three times if he loved Him, paralleling Peter's three denials, and with each affirmation of love, Jesus recommissioned him to feed and take care of His sheep (John 21:15-17). This exchange was not just a personal reconciliation but also a public restoration of Peter's role among the disciples.

This last gathering was significant for several reasons. First, it reinforced the reality of Jesus' resurrection. He was not a ghost or a vision; He ate with them, spoke with them, and could be touched. His presence confirmed the truth of His resurrection and the promise of eternal life for all who believe in Him. Second, it highlighted the importance of community and fellowship. Jesus chose to reveal Himself in the context of a shared meal, a setting familiar and intimate, emphasizing the communal nature of the Christian faith.

Furthermore, this gathering underscored the theme of forgiveness and restoration. Jesus did not abandon His disciples despite their failures but sought them out, offering them grace and a renewed purpose. This act of forgiveness is a model for the church, demonstrating that failure is not final, and that restoration is always possible with Jesus.

"The Last Get Together" by the Sea of Galilee serves as a powerful reminder of Jesus' love, His forgiveness, and His desire for fellowship with His followers. It teaches us that Jesus meets us in our everyday lives, inviting us into deeper relationships with Him and with each other.

Choosing a Successor

After the resurrection, one of the most significant moments between Jesus and His disciples occurred by the Sea of Galilee. Here, Jesus performed an act of profound grace and leadership; He appointed Peter as the rock on which He would build His church. This appointment was not just a mere passing of responsibility; it was an act of restoration for Peter, who had earlier denied Jesus three times before the crucifixion. This narrative beautifully illustrates how Jesus' forgiveness and trust can transform failure into a foundation for leadership and ministry.

The Gospel of John gives us a detailed account of this encounter. After a miraculous catch of fish, Jesus and His disciples gathered on the shore for a meal. It was in this intimate setting that Jesus addressed Peter directly. In a series of questions that mirrored Peter's threefold denial, Jesus asked Peter if he loved Him. Three times Peter affirmed his love for Jesus, and three times Jesus commissioned him: "Feed my lambs," "Take care of my sheep," and "Feed my sheep" (John 21:15-17). This repetitive questioning served not to condemn Peter but to reaffirm his role and heal the wound of his previous betrayal. This is how the story unfolds:

When they had finished eating, Jesus said to Simon Peter, "Simon son of John, do you love me more than these?" "Yes, Lord," he said, "you know that I love you." Jesus said, "Feed my lambs." Again Jesus said, "Simon son of John, do you love me?" He answered, "Yes, Lord, you know that I love you." Jesus said, "Take care of my sheep." The third time he said to him, "Simon son of John, do you love me?" Peter was hurt because Jesus asked him the third time, "Do you love me?" He said, "Lord, you know all things; you know that I love you." Jesus said, "Feed my sheep" (John 21:15-17).

This moment was significant for several reasons. First, it showed Jesus' willingness to forgive and restore those who have failed Him. Despite Peter's earlier denial, Jesus did not cast him aside but instead reaffirmed His trust in Peter. This act of restoration underscores the depth of Jesus' grace and the transformative power of His forgiveness. It reminds us that our failures are not the end of our story when we are willing to return to Jesus with a repentant heart.

Second, by appointing Peter as the leader of the early church, Jesus demonstrated His intentional plan for the continuation of His ministry on earth. Peter, once a simple fisherman, was transformed into a foundational figure in Christianity. Jesus' choice of Peter as His successor was a declaration of His confidence in Peter's faith and leadership, despite his flaws and failures. This choice also symbolizes the nature of Jesus' kingdom, showing that it is not reserved for the perfect but is built on the redeemed and restored.

Moreover, this event is a lesson in leadership and discipleship. Jesus' method of restoration and commissioning teaches us about the qualities of godly leadership. True leaders in the kingdom of God are not those who have never failed but those who have experienced the grace of God and are willing to lead others with humility, love, and a deep commitment to shepherd God's people according to His heart.

The Great Commission

Before His ascension, Jesus gathered His disciples one last time. This final meeting, charged with emotion and significance, took place near Bethany, where He bestowed a commission that would echo through the ages: "All authority in heaven and on earth has been given to me. Therefore go and make disciples of all nations, baptizing them in the name of the Father and of the Son and of the Holy Spirit, and teaching them to obey everything I have commanded you. And surely I am with you always, to the very end of the age" (Matthew 28:18-20). This Great Commission was not merely a set of instructions; it was a mandate to spread the Gospel across the earth.

This momentous instruction has profoundly shaped the trajectory of Christian evangelism and discipleship throughout history. The Great Commission begins with a declaration of authority. Jesus asserts that all authority in heaven and on earth has been given to Him. This proclamation establishes His divine sovereignty and legitimizes the command that follows. Jesus, as the risen Lord, holds ultimate authority, making His instructions binding and paramount for His followers.

The core of the Great Commission is the mandate to "go and make disciples of all nations." This directive emphasizes active engagement and movement beyond the confines of the immediate community. The term "nations" implies a global mission, transcending ethnic, cultural, and geographical boundaries. Jesus envisions a diverse, worldwide community of believers united in faith.

Integral to the process of making disciples are the acts of baptizing and teaching. Baptism, performed "in the name of the Father and of the

Son and of the Holy Spirit," signifies the initiation of new believers into the Christian faith, symbolizing purification and the beginning of a new life in Christ. Teaching involves instructing believers to obey everything Jesus has commanded. This encompasses not just intellectual knowledge but a holistic transformation of life and conduct in accordance with Jesus' teachings.

The Great Commission concludes with a comforting promise: "And surely I am with you always, to the very end of the age." Jesus assures His disciples that they will not be alone in this mission. His presence will accompany them, providing guidance, strength, and encouragement. This divine presence, mediated through the Holy Spirit, empowers believers to fulfill the Great Commission with confidence and resilience.

The Great Commission has been the driving force behind the global spread of Christianity. Throughout history, missionaries have ventured into unfamiliar and often hostile territories to proclaim the gospel, establish churches, and disciple new believers. The apostolic zeal inspired by the Great Commission laid the foundation for the early church and continues to animate contemporary Christian missions.

The Goodbye

After His resurrection, Jesus appeared to His disciples over forty days, teaching them about the kingdom of God and preparing them for the mission ahead. Now, it was time for His departure, as He prepared to ascend to heaven from whence He came. The account of Jesus' goodbye and subsequent ascension is not just a farewell; it embodies hope, promise, and the empowerment of His followers.

Jesus instructed them to stay in Jerusalem until they received the gift of the Holy Spirit. While the Bible does not specify that this instruction was given after the Great Commission, I include it here for continuity. It simply states, "[After the resurrection] He appeared to them [the disciples] over a period of forty days and spoke about the kingdom of God. On one occasion, while he was eating with them, he gave them this command: 'Do not leave Jerusalem, but wait for the gift my Father promised, which you have heard me speak about'" (Acts 1:3-4). This promise was fulfilled at Pentecost when the Holy Spirit descended upon the disciples, marking the birth of the Church and the beginning of a global movement that would transform the world.

As they stood on the Mount of Olives, Jesus blessed them and then ascended into heaven, a cloud concealing Him from their sight. The disciples watched in awe as Jesus was taken up before their very eyes (Acts 1:9). This moment was both a culmination of Jesus' earthly ministry and the commencement of His disciples' work as bearers of the Gospel.

The ascension of Jesus is significant for several reasons. Firstly, it signified the completion of His work on earth—His life, death, and resurrection had accomplished salvation for humanity. His ascension marked His return to the Father, where He now reigns as King and intercedes on behalf of His followers. Secondly, it marked a transition for the disciples. With Jesus no longer physically present, the responsibility fell on them to continue His work, empowered by the Holy Spirit, whom Jesus had promised.

The Ascension of Jesus is a pivotal event that encapsulates the true victory of Christ over the physical and spiritual realms. It is a testament to His divine nature and His eternal kingship, affirming that He lives and reigns with the Father, continuously advocating for us. For believers, this event is not merely historical but a profound assurance that Jesus is actively involved in our lives, guiding and empowering us through the Holy Spirit.

It reminds us that the work of the Gospel is ongoing, fueled by divine power and promise, calling each of us to participate in the grand narrative of redemption and eternal life. As we carry on His teachings and share His love, we are part of a divine mission, sustained by the knowledge that Jesus, our Lord, and Savior, will one day return to restore all things and reign forever.

The Promise of the Second Coming

As the disciples stood gazing upward, witnessing the ascension of Jesus, their awe and wonder were interrupted by an unexpected assurance from two men dressed in white, identified as angels. These messengers provided a cornerstone of Christian hope with their declaration: "Men of Galilee," they said, "why do you stand here looking into the sky? This same Jesus, who has been taken from you into heaven, will come back in the same way you have seen him go into heaven" (Acts 1:11).

This promise given by the angels is profound, painting a vivid picture of Jesus' return. It reassures believers that just as Jesus ascended visibly and bodily into heaven, His return will mirror this event—visible to all and in bodily form. The significance of this promise cannot be overstated; it anchors Christian hope in the tangible, historical, and future reality of Jesus' return. This second coming is not a spiritual metaphor but a future event that will completely fulfill God's plan for the world.

The angels' message at the ascension not only addresses the immediate confusion and awe of the disciples but also sets the stage for the Christian life. It transforms anticipation into action, directing the gaze of the disciples—and all future followers of Christ—from the skies back to the mission at hand. This promise encourages believers to live lives that reflect the values of Jesus' kingdom, actively engaging in the work of the Gospel while awaiting His return.

Jesus spoke of His return in several passages, perhaps most notably in the discourse on the Mount of Olives, where He described the signs that would precede His coming. He cautioned, "Therefore keep watch, because you do not know on what day your Lord will come" (Matthew 24:42). This admonition to "keep watch" is not a call to passive waiting but to active vigilance, living lives that reflect the values of His kingdom.

The assurance of Jesus' second coming propels Christians to maintain a posture of readiness and watchfulness. Jesus Himself taught about the importance of being prepared for His return, using parables to illustrate the necessity of vigilance and faithfulness (Matthew 25:1-13; Luke 12:35-48). The expectation of His return shapes how believers engage with the world, prioritizing love, justice, and the spread of the Gospel.

The promise of Jesus' second coming also offers comfort and hope, especially in times of suffering, injustice, and doubt. It assures believers that the current state of the world, with its pain and brokenness, is not the end of the story. There will be a day when Jesus returns to restore all things, to wipe away every tear, and to establish His reign of peace and justice forever (Revelation 21:4).

Establishing His Identity

A book on the 'Life of Christ' would be incomplete without a definitive exploration of who Jesus really was while on earth. Was He merely a teacher, a miracle worker, or something more profound? Skeptics often argue that He was nothing more than a moral teacher and certainly not divine, pointing out that He never explicitly said, 'I am God.' True, He never spoke those exact words, and for good reason. Instead, Jesus proved His divinity through His actions, teachings, and the fulfillment of Scripture, ensuring His audience could see beyond mere human abilities. He left no room for doubt about His identity. Let us explore how.

A pivotal aspect of Jesus' claim to divinity is his use of the title "Son of Man," deeply rooted in Old Testament prophecy. In Daniel 7:13-14, the "Son of Man" is described coming on the clouds of heaven, endowed with authority, glory, and sovereign power. When Jesus used this title, He was not merely identifying Himself as a human being; He was claiming a preordained, divine role that the religious audience of His time would understand as messianic and transcendent.

Furthermore, Jesus' use of the phrase "I and the Father are one" (John 10:30) was a direct assertion of His unity with God, stirring immediate and intense reactions from the religious leaders of the time. They picked up stones to stone Him, not because of a misunderstood metaphor, but because they recognized it as a claim to equality with God. This incident underscores that His contemporaries clearly understood Jesus' words as a claim to divinity, a fact often overlooked by modern skeptics.

Additionally, Jesus employed the sacred name of God, "I AM," in a context that unmistakably pointed to His eternal nature and divine essence. In John 8:58, Jesus declared, "Before Abraham was born, I am!" directly referencing God's self-identification in Exodus 3:14 as "I AM WHO I AM." This statement, made in the presence of religious scholars, was an explicit assertion of His existence as eternal and divine, linking Him directly to the God of their ancestors.

Jesus further proved His divine authority through His actions, particularly in His power to forgive sins, traditionally a divine prerogative. In Mark 2:5-12, Jesus not only healed a paralytic but forgave his sins, prompting the scribes to question, "Who can forgive sins but God alone?" Jesus' response, by highlighting His authority to forgive sins, publicly and palpably equated Himself with God.

Moreover, His resurrection is the cornerstone of His claim to divinity. The resurrection was not merely a miraculous event but a divine declaration and proof of His power over life and death, reinforcing His statements about His identity with tangible evidence.

In conclusion, although Jesus never simply stated 'I am God,' His declarations about His relationship with the Father, His fulfillment of prophecies, and His divine actions resoundingly affirm His divinity. Jesus articulated His divinity in ways that were culturally and historically profound, ensuring that His identity as God was unmistakably clear and leaving no room for ambiguity. He did not just hint at divinity; He demonstrated it in every aspect of His ministry, affirming that He was indeed the living God among His people. Jesus' life and words were not open to interpretation then, just as they are not now; they were a clear declaration of His divine nature and His eternal kingship.

Epilogue: The Journey Continues

As we reflect on the life of Christ, from the prophecy of His virgin birth to His miraculous resurrection and the promise of His second coming, we journey through a narrative that transcends time, culture, and understanding. This story, rich in divine intervention, profound teachings, and ultimate sacrifice, offers more than historical accounts; it presents a living invitation to experience the transformative love of God.

The life of Jesus Christ embodies the fullness of God's grace and truth. In His birth, we see the humility of the King of Kings, who chose to enter the world in the most humble circumstances. His teachings, parables, and miracles reveal a kingdom based on principles radically different from those of the world—principles of love, forgiveness, and self-sacrifice. Through His death, Jesus took upon Himself the weight of humanity's sin, offering redemption and the hope of reconciliation with God. And in His resurrection, we are given a living hope, a promise of new life that death cannot conquer.

The promise of Jesus' second coming further extends this hope, assuring us that the story is far from over. This promise encourages believers to live with anticipation and purpose, engaging the world with the love and truth of the gospel while awaiting the fulfillment of God's kingdom in its full glory.

As we stand in the present, the life of Christ compels us to look both backward in gratitude and forward in hope. Backward, to the cross, where the depth of God's love for us was displayed in stark reality. And forward, to the day of His return, when all things will be made new. In the meantime, our lives are to be lived in the light of His teachings and sacrifice, embodying the values of His kingdom as we serve, love, and share the good news with those around us.

This narrative, though ancient, speaks with urgency and relevance to our lives today. It challenges us to consider our response to the person of Jesus Christ—not just as a historical figure, but as the living Son of God, who invites us into a relationship with Him. It calls us to reflect on our own stories, how they have been touched by His grace, and how we can participate in His ongoing work in the world.

In the epilogue of our own lives, may we find that our stories have been woven into the greater story of God's love and redemption through Jesus Christ. And may we live in such a way that our lives echo the hope, love, and transformation found in Him, leaving a legacy that points others to the truth and beauty of the gospel.

The journey with Christ is one of continual growth, challenge, and deep joy. As we move forward, let us do so with hearts full of gratitude for the past, passion for the present, and hope for the future, secure in the knowledge that in Christ, we have eternal life.

A Note

While every precaution has been taken in the preparation of this book, the publisher assumes no responsibility for errors or omissions, or for damages resulting from the use of the information contained herein.

Also by Chris Morais

Kidney Cancer
The Life of Christ Jesus

About the Author

Chris Morais, MSc, MPhil, PhD, has been a medical research scientist for over three decades, specializing in Urology and Oncology. With a PhD in kidney cancer, Dr. Morais has published over 50 research articles, edited a scientific book, and mentored Honors, Masters, and PhD students. Through his scientific journey, Dr. Morais realized that while science addresses our mortal bodies, emotions, morality, and values transcend science. This led him to explore various religious texts for existential questions, ultimately finding answers in the Bible. He concluded, 'Science is for my perishable body, and Christ is for my immortal soul.' He writes to share biblical truths for the soul and medical knowledge for the body, explaining health conditions in simple terms without scientific or medical jargon.

www.ingramcontent.com/pod-product-compliance
Lightning Source LLC
LaVergne TN
LVHW051557070426
835507LV00021B/2622